# Separation–Individuation Struggles in Adult Life

*Separation–Individuation Struggles in Adult life: Leaving Home* focuses on the developmental task of separating from parents and siblings for individuals and couples who have not been able to resolve these issues earlier in life.

Sarah Fels Usher extends Mahler's theory, and includes the writing of Loewald and Modell, among others, stressing the right of adult patients to a separate life. She describes the predicament of Oedipal victors (or victims), their introjected feelings of responsibility for their parents, and their resultant inability to be truly individuated adults. Difficulties separating from siblings are also given analytic attention. Usher's experience treating couples adds a new and powerful dimension to her theory. She is optimistic throughout about the therapist's ability to help adult patients resolve the rapprochement sub-phase in a satisfying manner.

An additional, crucial question is raised when the author asks if the therapist can allow the patient to terminate treatment. Has the therapist achieved separation from their own parents – or, indeed, from their analyst? Exploring the plight of patients of the unseparated analyst, Usher describes how these generational factors rear their unfortunate heads when it is time to end therapy.

Listening to patients from the perspective of separation–individuation is not new; what is new is Usher's emphasis on how these particular issues are often masked by significant achievement in adult professional life. *Separation–Individuation Struggles in Adult Life: Leaving Home* will be of importance for psychoanalysts and psychoanalytic psychotherapists working with adults, as well as for clinical postgraduate students.

**Sarah Fels Usher** is a psychologist and psychoanalyst in private practice in Toronto, Canada. She is past president of the Toronto Psychoanalytic Society, Founding Director of the Fundamental Psychoanalytic Perspectives Program, and a faculty member of the Toronto Institute of Psychoanalysis. Dr. Usher is also the English language book editor of the *Canadian Journal of Psychoanalysis/Revue Canadienne de psychoanalyse*, and author of the Routledge titles *What is This Thing Called Love?* (2007) and *Introduction to Psychodynamic Psychotherapy Technique, 2nd Edition* (2013).

'This highly informative volume extrapolates Margaret Mahler's childhood separation–individuation paradigm to adult psychic development. Addressing major milestones of separation during adulthood and persistent conflicts around separateness, Usher's book becomes a powerful source of enhancing empathy on the part of parents, mentors, and clinicians for those under their care. This is a major achievement and deserves our appreciation and gratitude.'

**Salman Akhtar, M.D.,**
Professor of Psychiatry, Supervising and Training Analyst,
Psychoanalytic Center of Philadelphia.

'Bridging intra-psychic, interpersonal and socio-cultural perspectives, this book explores the complexities of separation, loss, and individuation in the context of the twenty-first century. Although self and object constancy are normally achieved antecedent to the Oedipal phase of development, aspects of separation–individuation process continue through the life cycle. Long after the onset of adulthood the internal need for a caring, protective parent persists, with significant influence on cognition, emotion, and behavior. Mental health professionals will find Sarah Usher's book to be a very informative, stimulating inquiry and integration.'

**Harold P. Blum, M.D.**

'Usher has produced yet another clinical gem. The down-to-earth charm of her abundant case reports embodies a significant theoretical integration of ego psychology, attachment theory, and self-psychology—without essentializing early development. Mahler's central infant conflict is reconceived as a cyclical life dynamic that also spans the generations. Bridging the gap between psychoanalytic psychotherapy and couples counseling, Usher shows us how to re-weave the present with our patients through the dimly known strands of their family histories.'

**Charles Levin, Ph.D.,**
Director, Canadian Institute of Psychoanalysis (Quebec English Branch),
Editor-in-chief, *Canadian Journal of Psychoanalysis.*

# Separation–Individuation Struggles in Adult Life

Leaving Home

Sarah Fels Usher

Routledge
Taylor & Francis Group

LONDON AND NEW YORK

First published 2017
by Routledge
2 Park Square, Milton Park, Abingdon, Oxon OX14 4RN

and by Routledge
711 Third Avenue, New York, NY 10017

*Routledge is an imprint of the Taylor & Francis Group, an informa business*

*British Library Cataloguing in Publication Data*
A catalogue record for this book is available from the British Library

*Library of Congress Cataloging in Publication Data*
Names: Usher, Sarah Fels, author.
Title: Separation-individuation struggles in adult life : leaving home / Sarah Fels Usher.
Description: Milton Park, Abingdon, Oxon ; New York, NY : Routledge, 2017. | Includes bibliographical references and index.
Identifiers: LCCN 2016007403 | ISBN 9781138658264 (hbk : alk. paper) | ISBN 9781138658271 (pbk : alk. paper) | ISBN 9781315620923 (ebk)
Subjects: LCSH: Separation-individuation. | Psychotherapy. | Developmental psychology.
Classification: LCC RC489.S45 U84 2017 | DDC 616.89/14--dc23
LC record available at http://lccn.loc.gov/2016007403

ISBN: 978-1-138-65826-4 (hbk)
ISBN: 978-1-138-65827-1 (pbk)
ISBN: 978-1-315-62092-3 (ebk)

Typeset in Times New Roman
by Saxon Graphics Ltd, Derby

For my parents

# Contents

# Acknowledgements

I want to thank Linda Mayers for reading an early draft of the first chapters; Ian MacKenzie of Paragraphics for his invaluable editorial assistance; Ehud Avitzur for his help with the title; and my colleagues Joseph Fernando, Anne Lazenby, Sharian Sadavoy, and Martha Wright for their encouragement throughout. My continually patient and supportive husband, Gary, provided exactly the right amount of separation during the writing of this book. Most of all, I thank my patients, whom I have had the privilege of treating and of learning from, and who are the source of my inspiration.

I also acknowledge Karnac Books, London, for permission to reprint parts of Chapter 3, originally published in *Hopelessness: Developmental, Cultural, and Clinical Realms* (2015), edited by Salman Akhtar and Mary Kay O'Neil. The New Yorker cartoon featured in Chapter 3 is reprinted with the kind permission of Christopher Weyant/New Yorker. The permission for the Lennon/McCartney lyrics at the beginning of the book was granted as follows:

**She's Leaving Home**
Words and Music by John Lennon and Paul McCartney
Copyright © 1967 Sony/ATV Music Publishing LLC
Copyright renewed
All Rights Administered by Sony/ATV Music Publishing LLC, 424 Church Street, Suite 1200, Nashville, TN 37219
International Copyright Secured. All Rights Reserved
*Reprinted by Permission of Hal Leonard Corporation*

# Introduction

*Separation–Individuation Struggles in Adult Life: Leaving Home* is about self-defining separation in later development: the external steps of leaving home – for university, a job, or relationship – and the complex intrapsychic leavings that involve an ongoing reorganization of shifting internal representations of parents and caretakers.

Issues of separation described here are dynamic and changing in our society, even as we revisit them: many adult children now leave home later or return more frequently after leaving, and they often marry later than people did in previous generations. This is partly the result of the economic realities of our time – the scarcity of jobs, the cost of housing – but it also seems to indicate a slowing of internal maturing and of separation from parents. Technology, including the use of communication methods such as Skype and texting, probably contributes to, or perhaps arises from, this slowing phenomenon, giving new meaning to the expression, 'Keep in touch'.

The experience of the adult 'child' in the process of separating from parents or former caretakers has been a compelling focus of my practice. I am aware of the risk of a tendency to see all my patients through this lens, as I begin to notice the prominence of separation problems in some of them. I have tried here to confine my focus to those for whom these problems seem to be a major stumbling block – usually, of course, in concert with other difficulties – in leading a satisfying life. I have seen a number of adults of different ages with remarkable – and one might say, ingenious – compromise formations, as they struggle to deal with leaving home, that is, separating from their families of origin. They present with panic attacks, painful somatic problems, depression, sometimes rage, difficulties in intimate relationships, and often a pervading sense of hopelessness, for example, 'This is my life. I'll never get free.'

It is notable how vast geographic separation – and even the death of a parent – may fail to alter the psychic struggle significantly, although it is usually modified under these circumstances. Anyone treating young adults, and even the middle-aged, in Western culture who live apart from parents as essentially separate beings, will be familiar with their patients' palpable anxiety and fear about losing their sense of self on a brief visit 'home', for example, for holidays. Yet, if the geographic separation is initiated by the parents – moving from the family home to a different city – protests about being smothered usually vanish almost instantaneously. Object relations is object relations, but the unconscious is the unconscious.

I have attempted here to formulate the issues involved in the often formidable task of leaving home, and to make psychoanalytic sense of them. Hearing the material only from my patients' viewpoint, it has sounded like a one-way street: 'My parent(s) won't let me go.' On the other hand, I hear my patients' longing not to be let go, to continue to be the beneficiary of their parents' or siblings' care, worry, and guidance, as in 'No one will ever care about you the way your mother does.' As Margaret Mahler herself says, the longing for the erstwhile good mother before separation remains with us throughout life. I have applied Mahler's theory describing early infancy, from hatching to the resolution of the rapprochement crisis and the attainment of object constancy, to work with the young and middle-aged adults I see in my practice. But this theory can only be stretched so far.

Shapiro (1993) writes, 'the Mahlerian idiom has fallen into relative disuse or is in dry-dock for repair' (p. 925). I have attempted here to take it out of dry-dock, applying Mahler's theory in her description of the stages of early infancy, from hatching to the resolution of the rapprochement crisis and the attainment of object constancy, to the young and middle-aged adults I see in my practice. These patients seem all to be stuck in one sub-phase – practising? rapprochement? They all have attained significant academic and professional status. In some cases, they even have mature, loving, adult relationships. But they remain bound to their family of origin in a way that feels incongruent with their contemporary life. Their experience, in some situations, is of being needed by a parent or parents – which, in some cases, has been strongly reinforced, of being bullied by a sibling or parent into very low self-esteem, and/or of such intense feelings of ambivalence about leaving home that their choices appear to be to merge or to murder. And the thing just won't budge. One feels like reassuring them that there will be more, and better, emotional refuelling after resolving the rapprochement crisis. But it is frightening for some otherwise very competent people to take what they see, or have been made to see, is the last step out. Sometimes it can be accomplished with a deep understanding of the conflicts that underlie it, sometimes with the help of a partner or sibling, sometimes in a desperate 'Me and Bobby McGee' way, as in 'freedom's just another word for nothing left to lose', when they fear the consequences of leaving home will be the loss of a parent's love. This failure-to-completely-launch phase, as I am calling it now, for want of a better name, is sometimes a patient's surprising secret revealed in therapy or in an intimate relationship. The 'transitional object' that is held onto is the person's memory of early unsatisfying relationships and their psychic representation of their place in the family.

Chapter 1 surveys the literature on separation, from Margaret Mahler, through attachment theory, including theories of self and relational psychology. The literature states that the type of personalities most susceptible to problems with leaving home are patients with masochistic tendencies; patients who have been abandoned in infancy (often a vague memory), or very early on; patients who were abused in some way by a parent; patients who hate and are burdened with the resultant unconscious guilt; patients who felt on the outside of their families and are desperate to be included in some way; and perhaps most importantly, patients who feel responsible for the care and 'entertainment' of their parent(s), those who sense the neediness in the parent(s) – those patients who are children of parents who can't let go.

Chapter 2 describes people trapped in these dilemmas who come for individual treatment and the effect this failure-to-completely-launch has on the degree of their maturity and success in life. This work is greatly enhanced by the analyst's helping patients to gain an understanding of their parents' histories, and thereby to understand more about the dynamics that affected their growing up. When the nature of the parents' need for attachment, for example, is better understood, this may ease the intensity of the guilt of leaving. As one patient put it, 'There doesn't have to be a *nuclear* explosion.' In the patient's transference to the analyst, I have found it helpful early on to notice their reaction to the perceived authority of the analyst. For example, an analysand asked me how much time was left in our session, despite the fact that a clock was placed where she could easily see it. She said she didn't think she was 'allowed' to look at the clock. In this case, the patient needed me to remain firmly as an authority, and manifested significant resistance to establishing the sense of a more equal partnership that might have made separation easier.

Chapter 3 gives examples of those who come for treatment in a couple, where failure-to-completely-launch issues for one or both partners can affect the relationship in insidious and sometimes blatant ways, and may even be fatal to it. In earlier generations, people often married in order to leave home. With more flexible norms, individuals can find ways other than marriage to use a romantic relationship for the same purpose. Still, most pathological separation issues do not resolve by marriage or coupling, as will become evident in the examples in this chapter.

The literature on siblings has just begun to grow and is discussed in Chapter 4, which focuses on the impact of sibling relationships on the progress through separation–individuation. This is a relatively new field of exploration, not discussed by Mahler and the early developmentalists. An overly close attachment to a sibling can lead to difficulties in growing up. An individual may fear, consciously or unconsciously, growing 'past' an older sibling, as in being more successful professionally or financially; or that by leaving home, they are abandoning a younger sibling who is left behind in a toxic environment. If a sibling has been erotized or idealized, the search for a romantic partner who is a replacement may result in feelings of betrayal of the original object. For example, inhibited sexual responsiveness in the new relationship may be due to unconscious incestuous fantasies and thus interfere with a person's full involvement in the connection that might help them to truly leave home. As well, a sibling with severe emotional difficulties that have been frightening and/or abusive may cause a person to become reserved or unable to trust, and therefore be inhibited in establishing a new bond outside the family. If a sibling – particularly an older sibling – has been persistently sadistic or repeatedly cruel and critical, the victim sibling may suffer a severe loss of self-esteem and perceive themselves as incompetent to face the challenges of life outside the family.

Chapter 5 deals with both treatment pauses and termination, that phase where the most important part of analytic treatment affected by the analysand's – and the analyst's – achievements, or lack thereof, in the area of separation comes to (real) life. Can the analyst let go? Can the analysand leave? In some situations, are patients exquisitely aware of the analyst's need for them? Early issues of leaving/separation rear their heads for both parties and may result in a defensive happy ending, a kind of psychic tug-of-war, or deep expressions of grief and loss. In many ways, the process of termination, and the patient's ongoing psychic life after termination, is the true test of the success of an analysis.

This book is a detailed record of what patients have taught me about their journeys of separation, and so the stories are from their perspective, as much as possible. There may appear to be too big a leap, almost a conflation of concepts, in my moving back and forth from infancy and toddlerhood (Mahler) to Oedipal time (Freud), and on to post-Oedipal time. I see separation as continuing throughout the lifespan, with some fluidity. Achieving separation-individuation and resolving the rapprochement crisis and oedipal frustrations and desires, magnified in adolescence, plays a significant role in adulthood. The book is limited to the stories of the adult 'children', rather than their parents' stories. The pain of separation from the point of view of parents as their children grow and leave the nest is referred to in comparison with the analyst–analysand dyad, and certainly deserves further study.

I hope the following will help us rethink what encourages or inhibits our patients' growing up and taking pleasure in life as adults. Freud's famous comment that a normal person should be able to *lieben und arbeiten*, to love and to work, with enjoyment, implies living as a separated/individuated adult.

This book – as does most of our psychoanalytic writing – leans heavily on the experiences and words of patients. The ages of the patients portrayed here are accurate, but for the sake of confidentiality, they have been described only as 'professional' in terms of their vocational lives; their exact area of work has not been elaborated. It has been a frustration for me, as it is for most analytic writers, that the examples discussed here cannot be described in detail, as these patients' achievements at work and other adult tasks contributed to the shock value of their positions vis-à-vis separation, and thus to the thesis of this book; however, even though the people involved here have given overall permission, their identities had to be protected.

In a series of articles, Kantrowitz (2004a, 2004b) describes the position of conflict in which analysts find themselves when writing about patients. 'They must protect the confidentiality of their patients while simultaneously providing clinical data accurate enough to support their ideas' (2004a, p. 70). In her research, Kantrowitz found that twice as many analysts surveyed used only the method of disguise, and did not ask patients for permission. I am in agreement that the writing – and certainly the request for permission – serves as a transference-counter-transference enactment that may rupture the analytic frame and has an effect, even if the patient has terminated treatment. Of course, consent is always tinged with remnants of wanting to please or derail the analyst, depending on the therapeutic interaction. In my experience, patients wanted to please me, to 'help' with the research. There is a fine balance between collaboration and exploitation. Most patients featured in this book were asked for permission, but it was hard for me to get past the feeling of having put them on the spot, no matter how worthy was my intention of developing psychoanalytic ideas and attempting to contribute to the way therapists listen to and formulate their patients.

## References

Kantrowitz, J. L. (2004a). Writing about patients I: Ways of protecting confidentiality and analysts' conflicts over choice of method. *Journal of the American Psychoanalytic Association*, 52, 69–99.

Kantrowitz, J. L. (2004b). Writing about patients III: Comparisons of attitudes and practices of analysts residing outside and within the USA. *International Journal of Psychoanalysis*, 85, 691–712.

Shapiro, T. (1993). A view from the bridge. *Journal of the American Psychoanalytic Society*, 41, 923–928.

*Wednesday morning at five o'clock as the day begins*
*Silently closing her bedroom door*
*Leaving the note that she hoped would say more*
*She goes downstairs to the kitchen clutching her handkerchief*
*Quietly turning the backdoor key*
*Stepping outside she is free*
*She (We gave her most of our lives)*
*Is leaving (Sacrificed most of our lives)*
*Home (We gave her everything money could buy)*
*She's leaving home after living alone*
*For so many years (bye bye).*

# Chapter I

# What we know so far

The moment Margaret Mahler, a Hungarian psychiatrist (1897–1985) met Sándor Ferenczi (also Hungarian) in high school, she was fascinated with the concept of the unconscious. She went on to study paediatric medicine in Vienna, became a child psychiatrist, and then, after an analysis with Helene Deutsch, became a psychoanalyst. And the rest, as they say, is history.

Blum (2004) informs us, from his personal communication with her, that Mahler's mother had been murdered at Auschwitz, 'an act she could neither forgive nor forget'. He goes on to say, 'Feeling unloved by her mother, who had very much favored her younger sister, Mahler was highly ambivalent toward her own mother yet immensely curious concerning mothers and their infants more generally' (p. 538).

The discussion of separation–individuation begins with Mahler's work. When she proposed the concept of separation–individuation, she described it, first, as occurring from the end of the first year of life through the second and third years, when the baby emerges from a complete, and supposedly blissful, mother–infant symbiosis. Seeing her theories as extending those of Freud, rather than being anti-Freudian, she studied babies and preschool normal and psychotic children, and demonstrated that there is life before Oedipus, and that life is significantly and amazingly interactive.

Mahler's results have been described in many important publications, most particularly *The Psychological Birth of the Human Infant* (1975), with Fred Pine and Annie Bergman, both psychologists, alive and well and living in Manhattan at the time of this writing. Mahler developed her formulations of the process of separation–individuation largely on the basis of the interplay of object relations and ego development (Blum, 2004). She defined separateness or separation as the intrapsychic achievement of a sense of separateness from mother and, through this, from the world at large. In her observations of how normal babies attain a sense of being separate individuals, within the presence of the caretaking mother, Mahler stated that the infant emerges from that blissful symbiosis through a series of steps, to become a separate human being with a sense of self and of the object. This process was referred to as 'hatching', calling up the image of a chick breaking free of the egg. When a baby begins to move around, Mahler said, it needs to explore the surrounding environment and yet to return to the mother for 'emotional or libidinal refuelling', a term coined by Furer (in Mahler, 1963). This brings the baby into the practising sub-phase – which Mahler thought started from about 10–15 months of age, and in which she describes the baby as elated. During this very important period, the baby has the excitement of exploration and mastery in the world, but still manages the feeling of being one with the mother. Importantly, for the purposes of this book, Bergman and Harpaz-Rotem (2004), working with Mahler, state that with careful filmed observation of babies and their mothers, they found that each developmental achievement of the baby changed the mother–child relationship.

Pine and Furer (1963) explain that, according to Mahler, normal separation–individuation takes place in the setting of a developmental readiness for, and pleasure in, independent functioning – made possible by the mother's presence. They further clarify that separation and individuation (concepts we often string together today) were originally conceived of as two complementary developments: separation, consisting of the child's emergence from the symbiotic fusion with the mother; and individuation, reflecting the achievement that marks the child's assumption of his own individual characteristics.

Akhtar (1994) points out that disruption is an integral aspect of psychic development and the psychoanalytic process. He states that the onset of a differentiated sub-phase disrupts the calm of symbiosis; the rapprochement sub-phase destabilizes the euphoric self-reliance of the practising phase. Analysts become aware of the function of disruption as the treatment of these patients progresses.

In this book, the work of Mahler and her co-investigators will be applied to contemporary clinical practice with adults. It seems to me that what we need at many points in our development – particularly during puberty and adolescence, but also as we lurch into adulthood – is exactly what Mahler describes with babies: the excitement of exploration and the availability of refuelling, of touching base. If a parent can move in and out at the 'right' times for the growing individual – at least most of the time – then separation and individuation can take place with a productive balance of disruption and caring. When we reach adulthood, parents are still needed – albeit more in the background – to provide support and, at times, guidance.

Many of us see adult patients who are in a kind of 'practising' sub-phase, or who are caught up in the struggle for individuation. What Mahler called 'ambitendency', alternatively a wish to be on one's own and to have mother present to provide solutions – sometimes only to reject them, the behaviour that culminates in the rapprochement crisis – can often be seen quite clearly in these adults. Bergman (1982) states that separateness not only becomes a cognitive perceptual reality but also has to be accepted emotionally. This realization results in the crisis that characterizes separation anxiety – the simultaneous wish for, and fear of, separateness and autonomy. For children, one cannot emphasize too strongly the importance of the optimal emotional availability of the mother during this (practising) sub-phase. 'It is the mother's *love* of the toddler and *acceptance of his ambivalence* that enable the toddler to cathect his self-representation with neutralized energy' (Mahler et al., 1975, p. 77; last emphasis mine).

Adults who have not experienced this acceptance, and for whom these earlier tasks were not achieved, are thrust into the demands of adulthood because of their chronological age. These patients often present with symptoms of phobias – particularly intense anxiety in areas that represent separation or independence, such as flying or learning to drive, and even agoraphobias (e.g. Katan, 1951); symptoms of achievement inhibition, i.e. in being all they can be – either at work or in their romantic relationships; and significant difficulties in negotiating their adult relationship with their parents or siblings. The lack of resolution of fantasies, passions, desires, and hatred linked to the Oedipal stage of life contributes to the inability to move forward. And they are weighed down by significant conscious and unconscious guilt.

Over half of adult patients I have seen in the last ten years have had problems growing up, particularly in separating from their families – parents, and, at times, siblings. In these cases, Mahler's later sub-phases experienced in separation–individuation seem to apply in spades – transposed to adulthood. I am thinking here particularly of the practising and rapprochement sub-phases, which lead to object constancy and self-constancy. Studying the task of boys versus girls in this arena, Bergman (1982) writes that the little boy is helped to separate by aligning himself with his father, and thereby he can more easily differentiate himself from his mother. He agrees with Freud that the boy has an extra motivator to separate from mother – that is, castration anxiety. As a result, Freud says, the resolution of the Oedipus complex may be less complete for girls. From these perspectives, we could think of our adult male patients as possibly having had an easier time of it, but we know this is not necessarily the case, especially when the father is absent and there is the opportunity for an unwished-for Oedipal victory.

A young man I saw in my practice some years ago was referred to me by his maternal aunt, who happened to be a psychologist. At 30 years of age, he was still very attached to his mother, who lived in a nearby city. His father had died when he was in his early teens, and since then his mother had made use of his empathic skills by regularly telling him about her life and her problems. Even though he had managed to move from his hometown, he was returning every weekend, or every second weekend, to see his mother who 'needed' him. He had no social life in either city, and certainly no sexual relationships.

As the therapy progressed, he revealed that he was most worried about a brain tumour, diagnosed in his mother about ten years previous. He thought that she could die at any time and imagined that his going home frequently would save her from this fate. When the time was right in the therapy, I asked him to find out the type of tumour she had. His mother brushed off his question at first, then finally gave him a complicated medical term. When he returned to treatment, we consulted my medical dictionary together and discovered that it was, in fact, a type of benign, non-life-threatening tumour. At this point in our therapy, my patient had begun to understand the function that this tumour was serving for him, and how the collusion with his mother ensured he would not have to face adult life. He allowed that bit of research to change his life. He moved through the emotions of relief, then anger at his mother, and then sadness for her, who had only her tumour – and him – to hang onto. He stopped visiting her so often and encouraged her to go out and start her own life. This story has a happy ending: my patient began dating in the city in which he lived, and married some time later (as evidenced by a photo he sent me), and his mother continued in her life. This patient's willingness to let go of the idea of his mother's tumour spoke to his own, previously buried, need to be free of that part of their relationship and to start his own life. His resolution of the rapprochement crisis had a good result for both of them.

In this example, the father was no longer available, and my patient became 'the man of the house', charged with the care of his mother. As we know, a father does not have to die for this to happen. Fathers can be unavailable through work, illness, or through not wanting contact with the mother or children. Also, a passive father who does not fight for his wife and his place in the family during his son's Oedipal time, and afterwards, can contribute to this kind of situation, as can an overly needy mother who does not have her husband's attention.

Still, Bergman (1982) and Mahler agree that separation–individuation is usually more difficult for girls. In reporting on research on the practising sub-phase in toddlers, Bergman (1982) found that girls have greater difficulty in resolving the rapprochement crisis than do boys. Boys were more able to turn away from the struggle with mother and invest their energy in the outside world; girls, on the other hand, became more enmeshed in the struggle – preventing them from focusing fully on the outside world. For girls, father has to be in the picture, says Bergman, but they must also hang onto their identification with mother. 'It is my impression that the girl's femininity and the impact on her of the sexual difference are closely connected with the mother's sense of herself as a woman and her feelings about her daughter as a girl ... in subtle ways, she communicates to her daughter what she wishes [*needs*] her to be' (p. 67). The old adage that a son is a son until he takes a wife, while a daughter's a daughter the rest of her life rings hauntingly true in terms of the expectations of both genders.

## Clinical vignette 1.1

Sue, a 35-year-old handicapped woman, who came for treatment because she had been suffering from panic attacks, was the first person to introduce me to the expression 'dutiful daughter'. Her parents had taken special care of her because of her handicap. Her mother did not trust her to organize her own apartment, or to be alone in the kitchen, and of course had never taught her to use make-up. Like many impaired people, Sue had figured out a way to satisfy her intellectual curiosity early on and completed university, eventually with a graduate degree. She had moved to a different city, but her mother came to 'take care of her' at least once a month. Sue also was the designated offspring to help her parents when they needed it, as her older brother was married and 'busy'. The panic attacks had started when her father had a heart attack. She feared he would die and then that her mother would not be far behind.

As Sue talked more about her family, she described herself as feeling like 'a sack of potatoes', as they planned who would drive her places and how she would fit into situations. The therapy was long and complicated, but in the area of separation, Sue made great strides. In the first phase, she allowed herself to become enraged at her parents for not trusting her competence, and soon did not want to see them at all; much later, she was able to enjoy seeing them and to look forward to their visits, which were less frequent than they had been in the past, and briefer, and were no longer for the purpose of taking care of her (her mother enjoyed shopping in the city). When we first talked about dating, Sue said she would have to 'move to Australia' to meet a man. One of her later fantasies involved meeting a man, getting engaged, and calling his parents, who could be heard cheering over the phone. They would not tell her parents, as she expected a cool reception. As she moved forward, Sue was able to see that, like her parents and her brother, she, too, was entitled to meet someone. When she came to one session with the song 'Defying Gravity' on her mind (she had printed out the words for me), we knew we were well on our way. In our understanding of her earlier fear (and panic attacks) regarding her parents' death, we were able to gradually bring the wish into consciousness, as she remembered an incident of her father exposing himself to her. Interestingly, Sue's resolution of the rapprochement crisis with her parents came before, and more naturally than, the resolution with her older brother. This will be elaborated in Chapter 4.

Winnicott (1990), a contemporary of Mahler, identified three categories of growth: absolute dependence, relative dependence, and towards independence. Evoking his now-famous phrase describing the processes of the infant as constituting a state of *going on being,* he writes that the mother's natural task is to protect this state in her baby. But relative dependence, he says, must include a gradual failing of adaptation. 'It is part of the equipment of a majority of mothers,' he states optimistically, 'to provide a graduated de-adaptation, which is nicely geared to the rapid developments of the baby' (p. 87). With healthy growth, 'what the infant needs is just what he usually gets [if he is lucky], the care and attention of someone who is going on being herself' (p. 88). Like Mahler's separation–individuation phase, Winnicott's stage of towards independence identifies the healthy child as gradually able to meet the world and all its complexities. He ends stating, 'Adults must be expected to be continuing the process of growing and of growing up, since they do but seldom reach to full maturity' (p. 92).

Meanwhile, John Bowlby (1907–1990), a British child psychiatrist and psychoanalyst, a young contemporary of Mahler, was observing how emotionally disturbed children's relationships with their mother affect their social, emotional, and cognitive development, and how children experience intense distress (crying, clinging, frantically searching) when separated from their mothers. He explicated his now well-known, and still much used, attachment theory, first in a report for the World Health Organization in 1951, defining attachment as a deep and enduring emotional bond that connects one person to another across time and space. In 1962, when the World Health Organization next focused on child care, Mary Ainsworth wrote a report that described and elaborated attachment theory. She set up a laboratory in which an artificially created situation – which she called 'the strange situation' – allowed for the observation, and then differentiation, of attachment patterns between mothers and infants: secure, anxious-resistant, and avoidant attachment behaviours. Her method has become an internationally recognized standardized method for evaluating the infant–mother relationship in terms of attachment.

Blum (2004) states that both Mahler and Bowlby had personal motivations for their research into separation and attachment: both had experienced maternal insensitivity and rejection. Mahler's personal influences were described earlier. Bowlby lost his nanny at 18 months, his governess at age 4, and was sent to boarding school at age 11 – all of which contributed to his later interest in problems of attachment, separation, and loss. In comparing separation–individuation theory and attachment theory, Blum (2004) states that both theories were initially regarded as diverging from traditional views. However, while Mahler remained loyal to the classical formulation and regarded her contributions as complementary to libido theory, Bowlby saw his theory of attachment as different from Freudian theory, independent of traditional biological instinct theory, psychoanalytical instinctual drive theory, and nutritional hunger. Mahler assumed attachment to the primary object, which she regarded as intrinsic to the process of separation–individuation. In comparing the two theories, Blum points out that attachment theory does not account for the essential development of separation–individuation, which is of prime importance for the promotion of autonomy, independence, and identity.

Blum agrees with Mahler that the path to object constancy, the final sub-phase of separation–individuation, is a major developmental milestone. He adds, further, that this concept, and Mahler's formulation of the process of separation–individuation, is not diminished by the importance, more recently, of attachment. 'Secure attachment in later life and object constancy are two sides of a complementary development … Attachment alone, without separateness and the formation of self- and object-representations, if at all conceivable would lead to developmental arrest' (2004, p. 546).

In his later work, Bowlby described attachment as characterizing human behaviour over the complete lifespan. Adult attachment research grew naturally from child research, with the Adult Attachment Interview being devised to measure adult attachment styles. This did not happen in the same way for separation–individuation theory. Although we could argue that the two theories are intricately related, Mahler's concepts seem to have been dropped in favour of the newer, shinier attachment theory, with its rather cumbersome, but impressive, interview.

In Blum's description of the limitations of attachment theory, he concludes that attachment theory disregards the dynamic unconscious, while separation–individuation theory was developed within psychoanalytic structural theory. 'The concept of separation–individuation, though currently marginalized by attachment and other object relations theories, remains an important contribution to our map of the preoedipal period' (2004, p. 551).

Bergman et al. (2013) agree. They relate separation theory and attachment theory in describing the early development of two sisters, each of whom was received differently by the same mother, who had not been ready to be a parent, and each of whom had a quite different, but problematic, relationship with her. The authors state that the daughter who had the most difficult relationship with their mother 'did not have to idealize her or be idealized by her', and that helped her to create her own independent life more successfully than the daughter who was joyfully received and doted upon.

Attachment theory informs us that it is significantly more difficult for a person who is anxiously attached, or in a state of disorganized attachment, to separate from parents. When parents or caretakers push the child to separate too early, the child may become anxiously attached and have great difficulty resolving separation in adulthood. For example, a colleague of mine was sent off to summer camp for eight weeks at the age of five. There was only one visitors' day, halfway through, when parents could inspect the newly tidied bunks and hear about the steak that campers had for their lunch just before the visit (the only time in the summer when steak was served). Sending children to camp was a status symbol in their social group – and, incidentally, produced a lot of excellent golfers among the parents. For her, this action led her to feel nobody cared at home, and she developed extreme anxiety and deep fears of abandonment in later life. Defensively, she became unnaturally independent at a young age, feeling she could not trust, or reliably take comfort in, a safe relationship with her parents. Similar difficulties may occur when young children are sent to boarding school, although in these situations, even in pre-adolescence, peers may substitute for parents, and often remain lifelong friends.

Mahler did not apply her theories to later-life separations, as she felt this would dilute the intrapsychic achievement of a sense of separateness at the core of the child's development, although she does acknowledge in several places that old conflicts over separation are reactivated later in life. She did postulate, however, that the longing for the symbiotic mother, who was 'part of the self' – and at one time was able to provide safety and well-being – was an existential aspect of human existence, and that this longing for the erstwhile all-good mother before separation remains with us throughout life. This highlights what a struggle separation from early caregivers can be. It shows itself at critical maturation points in adult life and quite clearly through the regression and transference in analysis. Fear of re-engulfment not only threatens a barely started individual differentiation but can also be a threat later in life, such as in romantic relationships and even in friendships.

Because there is very little specific literature on separation in adults, I have often found myself stretching the infant and child literature. Still, as stated in the introduction, the crossover between the separation–individuation phase and the Oedipal phase represents a critical intersection, with both remaining residually in various degrees throughout life. The following articles are welcome exceptions to those concerned with infant–parent relationships.

Blos (1967) described a second individuation process in adolescence, which includes shedding family dependencies and loosening infantile object ties in order to become a member of society. He states that individuation means that the growing person takes increasing responsibility for what he does and what he is, rather than expecting parents to take responsibility for him. The processes that we know about in adolescence – shifting of one's allegiance and idealization from parents to peer group, and often to public 'idols' who appear to proclaim the newly acquired values of the peer group – have been well documented.

Colarusso (1990, 1997, 2000) has also seen development as a lifelong experience. In his papers describing the third individuation, ages 20–40; the fourth, ages 40–60; and the fifth, ages 60 and beyond, he has attempted to understand the sexual and aggressive drives, object relationships, and environmental influences that affect the evolution of the ego and superego throughout the adult years. He states that adults do not repeat the original separation–individuation process as it occurs in the first three years of life, and that they are not, for the most part, involved in the differentiation of self from object. I do not agree with him here, as I have seen adult patients so merged with a parent that differentiation is quite difficult to achieve. I also do not agree with his thesis that individuations in adulthood are 'qualitatively different from the first ones in that they are characterized by interactions with individuals other than primary objects' (2000, p. 1471). I think this is only partly the case, as the new object relations derive from the primary ones, as we know, and although they are seldom as intensely cathected as the originals, there are times when the original object relations still dominate the person's landscape.

Earlier, Anny Katan (1951) introduced the term *object removal* when describing the separation–individuation stage of adolescent development, and differentiated it from *displacement:* 'In displacement, incestuous features (libidinous love for the parent) are retained; the concept of removal should be reserved for that process which abolishes incestuous tendencies once and for all. By this step the adolescent has grown up, i.e., he has acquired the ability to love as an adult' (p. 49). Katan adds that once this has been achieved, the individual never turns back – hence the object has been removed from its former place in the psyche. This seems extreme, as there are times in life when we wish to reconnect with those early objects in a deeply emotional way; this can be a measure of how successful separation and individuation have been.

The thesis in this book is that many adult individuations, if not all, are still concerned with the real objects of youth. And in some ways, Mahler agrees. In her early writing, she observes, 'I have maintained a rather personal interest in one specific aspect of the rich heritage that Freud bestowed on us, namely his emphasis on the fact that a lifelong, albeit diminishing, emotional dependence on mother is a universal truth of human existence' (Mahler, 1963, p. 307).

Heinz Kohut (1913–1981), who also lived at around the same time as Mahler, developed a theory of the self (1977), which, among other important tenets, stressed that we need certain kinds of input from individuals close to us – he used the term *self-objects* to describe them – in order to achieve and maintain cohesion, boundaries, vitality, and balance. His clear statement that these needs are not restricted to early development, but remain throughout life, was new for psychoanalysis. For Kohut, adult self-object needs were analogous, if not identical, to similar needs that exist in relation to the primary objects of infancy and childhood. If these needs for mirroring and idealizing responses from others are not met because of some failure in the child's environment, it can lead to a deficit in the individual (Levine, 1994). The fact that these needs *persist into adulthood* is consistent with the thesis of this book. Adults still need self-objects; one of the problems seems to be whether the objects that are being used are still the primary objects. Recognizing and integrating these needs in a healthy way as we mature is one of the tasks of growing up. Different from Mahler and Freud, but like Colarusso and Katan, Kohut saw the object of an individual's dependency as changing from mother to others in later adult life. However, he stressed that the need for mirroring and idealizing remains, more in some individuals than in others.

In terms of early and later stages in the development of adult independence, the work of Modell, Loewald, and Erreich, described below is extremely relevant, expressing so elegantly the issues of separation in adulthood.

Modell (1965) identifies the severe inhibition of development and growth that comes from an individual's feeling that they have no right to a separate adult life. He links this to the concepts of negative therapeutic reaction and unconscious guilt. Modell describes his patients who 'were possessed of a basic belief that they had no right to a better life' (p. 324) and proposes that the guilt that underlies these feelings relates to the belief that one does not deserve the kind of life that would hopefully come from a successful analysis; sometimes leading to a negative therapeutic reaction. He takes this theory further, to say that patients may also think that a successful outcome for themselves necessitates the depletion of others. This idea of an economy of success is present in the unconscious of many of our patients.

Loewald (1979) connects very clearly to the thesis of this book. He refers to Freud's concept of the turning away from the Oedipus complex as 'more than a repression' and states that, when ideally carried out, it amounts to a destruction and abolition of it.

> First: no matter how resolutely the ego turns away from it and what the relative proportions of repression, sublimation, 'destruction' might be, in adolescence the Oedipus complex rears its head again, *and so it does during later periods in life*, in normal people as well as in neurotics.
>
> (Loewald, 1979, p. 753; my emphasis)

Loewald introduces the term *parricide* in connection with this destruction, referring to the destruction of the parent by the child. Freud's focus on the Oedipal myth was the original reference to the killing of the parent/father. Loewald defines parricide as occurring in 'one who murders a person to whom he stands in a specially sacred relation, as a father, mother' (p. 755). From what seems to us now as a very ordinary example, Loewald formulates an important interpretation and conclusion. His patient was unable to finish his thesis, which was in the same academic field as his father's. He listens to his patient's ambitions and fears about outdistancing his father, and his guilt about these ambitions: 'It is no exaggeration to say that the assumption of responsibility for one's life and its conduct in psychic reality is tantamount to the murder of the parents, to the crime of parricide, and involves dealing with the guilt incurred thereby' (1979, p. 757). In other words, in some manner – metaphorically but honestly – we must kill our parents in order to become separate beings. See, for example, in the above description, where my patient Sue felt she would have to move to Australia to date a man – in an unconscious attempt to avoid committing murder. Loewald's idea certainly broadens Mahler's concept of 'hatching'.

'Honour thy father and thy mother: that thy days may be long upon the land that the Lord thy God giveth thee' (the Fifth Commandment, Exodus 20:12). God came before Loewald, after all, and before Freud. This is the conflict to which we are all subject: we must honour our parents, but we have to 'kill' them to survive as independent people.

> We are faced with a double paradox. Self-responsibility, involving parricide in psychic reality and in symbolic form ... is ... a crime ... But it is not only a crime of which humans inevitably become guilty in the process of emancipating individuation ...; self-responsibility at the same time is the restitutive atonement for that crime. Without the guilty deed of parricide there is no autonomous self ... To live among these paradoxes seems to be our fate for the time being.
>
> (Loewald, 1979, p. 761)

Loewald adds that in our role as children of our parents, through genuine emancipation, we do kill something vital in them – not all in one blow, and not in all respects, but we contribute to their dying. As parents of our own children, we have the same fate, unless we diminish them.

The concept of guilt is inherent as we talk about murder. 'If, without the guilty deed of parricide there is no individual self worthy of that name, no advanced internal organization of psychic life, then guilt and atonement are crucial motivational elements of the self' (Loewald, 1979, p. 761). Perceived in this way, guilt is not something to be eliminated, but constitutes a driving force in the organization of the self, and we must bear and master it by 'internalizing atonement' (p. 758).

I recently saw a woman in her fifties who expressed a dread of leaving home to travel, but she reported that after she arrived at the new place, she felt fine. As she talked about her life, an interesting story emerged: four weeks after her elaborate wedding, which cost so much that her father had to cash in his insurance policy, her father died of a burst aorta. Her mother, who suffered from depression, was destitute (no insurance) and killed herself some months later. That this patient was punishing herself for the separation action of getting married – which, in her mind, led to the deaths of both her parents – became evident early in the treatment. She had seen travelling as the ultimate pleasure. Also, of course, travelling is linked to leaving. Even though, or because, she now had some understanding of this association, she found it difficult to remain in treatment and often left for months at a time. However, she always came back, taking the steps toward working through her guilt at the only pace she could allow.

Erreich (2011) examined the forms of guilt with which those of us who do not suffer from personality disorders are burdened: Oedipal guilt, survivor guilt, and separation guilt, all of which she states are intermingled throughout life with our formation of a separate self. Although the patient she writes about is only five years old, her description gives us hope for understanding the often confusing guilt we see when treating adults struggling with separation.

Erreich states that much of classic psychoanalytic thinking about the Oedipus complex is centred on castration; that is, a fear of being harmed. To follow Modell's and Loewald's arguments, the notion of separation guilt represents a shift from fear of harm to a fear of harm*ing,* that is, harming by abandoning the loved object – beginning even in the pre-Oedipal period (an elaboration of Mahler's concept of ambitendency). Her patient, Nick, talked about a fantasy dog named Rover, who at times was inseparable from Erreich. 'At one point, after Nick made a dog license that would attach us to each other, I commented that this way Rover would never leave me. Nick surprisingly replied that Rover, in fact, wanted to get away from me, that Rover liked me but sometimes dogs want to be on their own' (2011, p. 132). Erreich's termination with Nick, described in Chapter 5, fit with the theme of Nick's wanting to leave but also being careful to protect Erreich. She concludes, 'This unconscious fantasy – "I can't (grow, progress, succeed) because if I did, I would feel too guilty" – is the link between fear of being abandoned by the object and guilt over wishes to separate' (p. 143).

That this idea is usually unconscious is significant. Sometimes patients can see this trend in their behaviour, but until they realize how deep it lies, and how strongly it drives their actions – and inaction – they cannot begin to absolve themselves from their guilt of leaving parents behind. Oedipal conflicts manifest themselves as obstacles to growing up, to leaving home in the real – not the virtual – sense, as passion turns to guilt, not for Oedipal desires, but for the rage felt by the individual because of the conflicted feelings of responsibility for the parents, of needing the parents, and of the desire to separate.

The *Concise Oxford Dictionary* defines rapprochement as a re-establishment or recommencement of harmonious relations. Loewald (1979) aptly describes the resolution of the rapprochement crisis, 'What will be left, if things go well, is tenderness, mutual trust, and respect'

(p. 758). Seeing patients who suffer from a failure to completely launch may involve us in informing our patients about – nay, selling them on – this pot of gold at the end of the crisis. Separation, even from needy, ill, or depressed parents, does not mean the end, but can bring about the beginning of refinding a relationship, this time between two adults who are free to love and care for each other as honestly as possible, and who have found a way to enjoy spending time together – for the most part. This revised version of rapprochement in adults comes only after they have accepted their right to a life.

Parents play a substantial part in their child's resolution of rapprochement in order for it to 'take'. Mahler and Pine's studies found that parent–child communication was extremely important for the successful achievement of normal individuation. The very young child can sustain some degree of separation from the parents only if he can contact them and communicate when he needs to. Therefore, the parents need to be available. 'One cannot emphasize too strongly the importance of the optimal emotional availability of the mother during the [rapprochement] subphase. It is the mother's love of the toddler *and acceptance of his ambivalence* that enable the toddler to cathect his self-representation with energy' (Mahler et al., 1975, p. 77; my emphasis).

As Mahler so accurately states, the parent's attitude depends on her or his own level of adjustment. If the parent can be quietly available with a ready supply of object libido and share in the toddler's adventuring exploits, the toddler will develop in a healthy way during early separation–individuation, and with a minimum of guilt.

Settlage (1994) states that parental influences are extremely critical in successful or failed separation. He identifies one form of influence that can result from parental '*failure to sanction and encourage separation–individuation*' (p. 29; emphasis in the original). This kind of failure will perpetuate dependency rather than encouraging growth toward autonomy, and can be shaped by the inadequate achievement of separation–individuation during the parents' own development. The consequence of this is that the parent has an 'intolerance for loss of relationship and a readily mobilized separation anxiety. There is a tendency to hold onto the child' (p. 29).

The excessive need to control the child may reflect not only the parent's difficulties with separation but also their own lack of modulated self-control. In one form, Settlage states, this need causes the parent to intrude on the child's spontaneous, autonomous, appropriately assertive behaviour. In another form, the parent may take unnecessarily stringent, disciplinary action. Or, perhaps even more terrifying, the parent's need to control may cause him or her to withdraw from the child into emotional unavailability. In a pathological but frequent outcome, the child seeks to regain the relationship by becoming compliant and submissive by subverting feelings and impulses, which can be evidenced in the formation of a false self (Winnicott, 1960). Patients may comply with the demands of needy parents by tailoring their own ambitions to fit what they perceive will not hurt their parents in any way. This tailoring is usually unconscious and can be seen quite clearly in the transference.

Thus, the often joyful parents must be prepared, or must prepare themselves, for a major, sometimes painful, transition in the relationship with their beloved offspring. 'As we learned rather late in our study, the emotional growth of the mother in her parenthood, her emotional willingness to let go of the toddler – to give him, as the mother bird does, a gentle push, an encouragement toward independence – is enormously helpful. It may even be a sine qua non of normal (healthy) individuation' (Mahler et al., 1975, p. 79). Although the early researchers mentioned the significance for the normal mother of her child's increasing individuation, and indicated that self-preparation was needed for separation as the child grows older, unfortunately, they did not go into detail and there seems to be no psychoanalytic writing in this area. There are occasions when I have been involved in the treatment of an older couple whose presenting problem includes the stresses of adult children who have not separated. For example, in the situation of one couple I treated, both partners' family histories were problematic in the area of separation: the husband's parents had been overcontrolling, while the wife's mother hadn't spoken to her in some years. They argued a great deal in our sessions about the amount of their time their 'children' needed. As we talked in depth about their relationship issues, we found ourselves exploring how their children exploited them. The husband actually kept track of the number of days they saw their children and grandchildren – providing babysitting, meals, and rides for them – during the therapy. With this evidence, he accused his partner of avoiding the couple time he said he needed. We could say they were now suffering from their earlier lack of encouraging their children to leave home. The therapy helped them to understand and strengthen their own relationship, and then to be able to decide on appropriate family time.

In many cases, parents' intellectual knowledge, and even contemporary psychological understanding, of their children's changing and growing does not seem to carry over to their emotional response, and ultimately, their behaviour. Information on helping parents to understand why it is so hard to let go, and how to let go in a nuanced manner – with as little as possible of the envy and anger that can result, on both sides, in clinging or outright abandoning – might be useful reading if anyone chose to write it.

In an article on agoraphobia, Milrod (2007) states that the underlying inner restriction in patients with panic disorders is striking. A panic disorder affects one's ability to think independently and to lead an emotionally full and intellectually broad and stimulating internal life. 'These patients do not feel competent or capable of leaving their designated "safe" spaces alone; often they feel comfortable only with a designated protector … upon whom they feel their safety depends' (p. 1009). In her clinical examples, she writes of patients who have a deep terror of being separate. Their parents were habitually blind to the fact that they were separate individuals, with their own emotional needs. The agoraphobia effectively prevented them from escaping their families, and becoming, in this case, separate beings.

Kramer (1979) states that the frame of reference we derive from our knowledge of developmental concepts, including the residues of preverbal and pre-Oedipal conflicts in our patients, makes those conflicts less burdensome and easier to cope with and can be used to enrich the analysis by the analyst who understands and even anticipates such regressive behaviour. In one case, she describes separation–individuation transference phenomena in a patient with fairly severe pathology, whose early practising sub-phase aroused some pride in her parents. The father left the home during the sub-phase proper, which caused her explorations to be curtailed. Kramer explains that the formation of a therapeutic alliance took a long time, and that this patient had difficulty entering and leaving the office.

Does the fear of or guilt about separation in adulthood apply only to individuals who have never gone through a 'proper' separation–individuation phase as toddlers? The answer seems to be a provisional yes, even if the separation crisis manifests itself in what seems to be a 'first episode' at later critical points in development, for example, leaving home for university or marriage. Pine (2004) cautions us that later adult phenomena cannot confirm specific hypotheses about early development, because our information is based on referring back to the patient's remembered history. He states that his clinical experience and the uses he has made of Mahler's concepts 'give no direct backing to her conception of a normal symbiotic phase or of the subphases of separation–individuation' (p. 528). However, he acknowledges the fruitfulness of the ways of thinking that underlie these hypotheses. Certainly we cannot ever know for sure – at least with the technology now at our disposal; however, Mahler's (and Pine's) work allowed for an organization of the cases presented here that made sense of certain adult manifestations of earlier separation problems.

In the following chapters, the anguish of adults who are caught in separation conflicts will be described in detail as they are observed in everyday clinical practice. Mahler's theories, along with the more recent research, will be applied to work with adults, in a contemporary way, as these conflicts are seen to show themselves at later critical developmental junctures. Certain individuals – not patients with extreme pathology, but people who may seem to be functioning well otherwise in life – may hit a wall when, for example, they try to excel professionally or to become involved in a deeply intimate relationship. In early adulthood, how much to-and-fro contact with parents, if they are available, does a young person need in order to separate – again – and become an individual? What seems to be most important is the patient's ability to feel entitled to their own life and the parents' ability, or lack thereof, to empathically follow the needs of their maturing and mature offspring.

Kramer (1979) states that greater knowledge and integration of developmental concepts and of the frame of reference of separation–individuation will add to the analyst's richer insights and more complete interpretations and reconstructions. 'Separation–individuation theory encompasses and organizes findings from many sources, research and clinical, and permits us to perceive and process material in a multifaceted way' (pp. 260–261).

The next chapter will outline situations where a failure to completely launch was presented in individual treatment. In Chapter 3, the interference of these failures for one or both partners in a couple is described. The effects of sibling relationships on separation–individuation are discussed in Chapter 4.

As was stated in the introduction, these chapters deal solely with those aspects of my patients' complaints that illustrate specific developmental issues, and thus they represent only a portion of their stories. Literature will be described as it relates to the focus of each chapter.

## References

Akhtar, S. (1994). Needs, disruptions, and the return of the ego instincts: Some explicit and implicit aspects of self psychology. In S. Kramer and S. Akhtar (Eds.), *Mahler and Kohut: Perspectives on development, psychopathology, and technique* (pp. 97–116). Northvale, NJ: Jason Aronson.

Bergman, A. (1982). Considerations about the development of the girl during the separation–individuation process. In D. Mendell (Ed.), *Early female development*. Richmond, VIC, Australia: Spectrum Publications.

Bergman, A. and I. Harpaz-Rotem. (2004). Revisiting rapprochement in the light of contemporary developmental theories. *Journal of the American Psychoanalytic Association, 52*(2), 556–570.

Bergman, A., I. Blom, and D. Polyak. (2013). *Attachment and separation–individuation issues: Two ways of looking at the mother/infant relationship.* Paper presented at the International Psychoanalytic Association Congress, Pribor, Czech Republic, August 4–7, 2013.

Blos, P. (1967). The second individuation process of adolescence. *Psychoanalytic Study of the Child, 22*, 162–186.

Blum, H. P. (2004). Separation–individuation theory and attachment theory. *Journal of the American Psychoanalytic Society, 52*(2), 535–553.

Colarusso, C. A. (1990). The third individuation: The effect of biological parenthood on separation–individuation processes in adulthood. *Psychoanalytic Study of the Child, 45*, 179–194.

Colarusso, C. A. (1997). Separation–individuation processes in middle adulthood: The fourth individuation. In S. Akhtar and S. Kramer (Eds.), *The seasons of life: Separation–individuation perspectives.* Northvale, NJ: Jason Aronson.

Colarusso, C. A. (2000). Separation–individuation phenomena in adulthood: General concepts and the fifth individuation. *Journal of the American Psychoanalytic Association, 48*(4), 1467–1489.

Erreich, A. (2011). More than enough guilt to go around: Oedipal guilt, survivor guilt, separation guilt. *Journal of the American Psychoanalytic Association, 59*(1), 131–151.

Katan, A. (1951). The role of 'displacement' in agoraphobia. *International Journal of Psychoanalysis, 32*, 41–50.

Kohut, H. (1977). *The restoration of the self.* Chicago: University of Chicago Press.

Kramer, S. (1979). The technical significance and application of Mahler's separation–individuation theory. *Journal of the American Psychoanalytic Association, 27S*, 241–262.

Levine, H. B. (1994). Mahler and Kohut: A comparative view. In S. Kramer and S. Akhtar (Eds.), *Mahler and Kohut: Perspectives on development, psychopathology, and technique.* Northvale, NJ: Jason Aronson.

Loewald, H. W. (1979). The waning of the Oedipus complex. *Journal of the American Psychoanalytic Association, 27,* 751–775.

Mahler, M. S. (1963). Thoughts about development and individuation. *Psychoanalytic Study of the Child, 18,* 307–324.

Mahler, M. S., F. Pine, and A. Bergman. (1975). *The psychological birth of the human infant.* New York: Basic Books.

Milrod, B. (2007). Emptiness in agoraphobia patients. *Journal of the American Psychoanalytic Association, 55*(3), 1007–1026.

Modell, A. H. (1965). On having the right to a life: An aspect of the superego's development. *International Journal of Psychoanalysis, 46,* 323–331.

Pine, F. (2004). Mahler's concepts of 'symbiosis' and separation–individuation, revisited, reevaluated, refined. *Journal of the American Psychoanalytic Association, 52,* 511–533.

Pine, F. and M. Furer. (1963). Studies of the separation–individuation phase: A methodological overview. *Psychoanalytic Study of the Child, 18,* 325–342.

Settlage, C. F. (1994). On the contribution of separation–individuation theory to psychoanalysis: Developmental process, pathogenesis, therapeutic process, and technique. In S. Kramer and S. Akhtar (Eds.), *Mahler and Kohut: Perspectives on development, psychopathology, and technique* (pp. 17–52). Northvale, NJ: Jason Aronson.

Winnicott, D. W. (1960). The theory of the parent–infant relationship. *International Journal of Psychoanalysis, 41,* 585–595.

Winnicott, D. W. (1990). *The maturation processes and the facilitating environment: Studies in the theory of emotional development.* London: Karnac.

# Chapter 2

# Oedipal victor or victim
## Individuals

The following three chapters tell the stories of patients I have met in the most recent ten years of my practice, all from a specific perspective: their problems with separation–individuation in adult life. It is interesting to keep in mind, as Bergman and Harpaz-Rotem (2004) remind us, that in terms of the infant–mother dyad, Mahler felt strongly that the *infant* had to carry the lion's share in the process of development. This chapter introduces the reader to detailed therapeutic work with two individuals, in particular, who will be followed throughout the course of the book.

## Clinical vignette 2.1

I first met Carla when she was 18 years of age and in her last year of high school. She was achieving top marks but was suffering from hair loss, insomnia, and intrusive obsessional thoughts. Carla stated that academic expectations from both her parents were very high.

### Parents' history in brief

Carla's father came from a large, religious family living in a sparsely-populated community in Canada, where there had been strict rules about how to conduct one's life. He was the only one of his six siblings who had left their small town and who had married outside his religion. Nevertheless, he kept in close contact with his family, visiting them with his new family at Christmas and during summer holidays. Carla's mother was from a disorganized family overseas. Her mother's father had abandoned the family when she was ten years of age. She had felt confused and unloved and had left home at the age of 16 to work in another city. She had so distanced herself from her family of origin that she had taught herself to speak without their accent. She eventually continued her university training independent of her family of origin and never had contact with them again. She became an integral part of her husband's family, which was the family Carla knew when she was growing up.

During Carla's early years, her mother, who often defended against her anxiety with the use of avoidance, spent many daylight and evening hours at a demanding job, leaving Carla to be cared for by her father who, being a writer, had more flexible time. Carla's father became the main nurturing parent. Carla also had a sister, nine years her senior, who had left home when she was 16 years of age, following in her mother's footsteps, and lived abroad with very little contact with the family. Carla's father was an alcoholic; his drinking, she recalled, was mostly under control during the day. Still, as she matured, Carla had the unfortunately typical experience of children of alcoholics of pouring alcohol down the drain, and of not wanting to invite friends to her home because she feared her father's behaviour would be embarrassing. Because her mother was so often absent, and her sister had left home, Carla became her father's partner at social events, which she sometimes found uncomfortable.

### Early treatment

After several months of psychotherapeutic treatment, Carla's initial symptoms of anxiety began to ease enough to allow the focus of our work to be on the critical juncture she was now facing: graduating from high school and applying to university. Should she leave home? She feared she would worry constantly about her father's health and mood if she went away. We had several discussions about the developmental tasks of adulthood. Using the word *task* was helpful with Carla, as it implied something that is expected of her, something she 'should' do, and Carla usually did what she should.

Just before the application deadline, Carla was able to choose a university out of town, not very far from home, bringing this phase of the therapy to a close. I did not hear from her during her four years away. When she returned, I learned that while she was away at university, she developed her first romantic relationship. She had invited her boyfriend home for a weekend to meet her parents. Her father was shocked and surprised that she would bring this man home and expect to sleep with him. He abruptly left the home for several hours and then withdrew from her completely for several months. Thus ended the relationship with the first boyfriend. Mother was noticeably absent from this story.

*Middle treatment*

After some months of our working together in this phase, Carla was accepted into graduate school, again away from home, a little farther this time, and I heard from her next when she was in her final year. She called to say she was extremely anxious, having 'crazy' thoughts, and that her hair was falling out again. Then she said, 'But my boyfriend doesn't mind.' She planned to return home after graduating, get a job, and find her own place to live. This boyfriend lived in her hometown.

We began meeting as soon as she returned. Her mother had set up consultations with dermatologists and neurologists for the hair loss, which at this point Carla was able to laugh about, suspecting the real cause. We settled in to discuss her new relationship.

Carla's boyfriend worked in the company where she had spent the previous summer. She was very flattered that he had taken a liking to her – and in fact, he had pursued her through her last year of graduate school. He had given her a reason to return home. He was significantly older than her, and as Carla got to know him better, she discovered that he also had a drinking problem, which she had not allowed herself to acknowledge earlier. As their relationship progressed, she found herself frequently helping him home after an evening out together. Carla introduced this boyfriend to her father who, perhaps seeing himself all too clearly, was able – in a more mature manner than he had previously – to tell Carla that this boyfriend was not the right person for her, and that she should end the relationship.

In our sessions in this phase, Carla came to understand her strong attachment and loyalty to this boyfriend as a resurfacing of her love, gratitude, and feelings of being taken care of by, and caring for, her father. After some time, she was able to end this relationship, but not without great pain. Her symptoms eased almost immediately. By now, she was enjoying looking for interpretations of her symptoms and behaviour. To foreshorten many months of therapy about this and other significant issues, I can report that some time later, Carla met another man, a graduate student her own age. He was of a different race, and she worried about introducing him to her parents – particularly, of course, her father. The meeting went much better than anticipated. Her father accepted him, and in fact, grew to like him, thankful that the old boyfriend was gone. Still, he kept fighting hard for her exclusive attention. At the end of one family meal that included the new man, he kept Carla back and asked many questions about her work. He had saved articles from the newspaper that he thought would help her. 'He's a great dad!' she said to me, expressing her deepest hope.

As a side note, it is interesting to ask if marrying a person from a different race or religion gives people the illusion that they are separating from their original families. A partner's external appearance and professed beliefs may assist at first, consciously. However, as the layers of the onion peel away (to use Freud's expression), individuals realize that their partner has all the important (sometimes negative) traits of the parent with whom they have the strongest enmeshment.

Carla eventually moved in with her new partner, but not without the following piece of a dream: '*I had a dream that everyone was cheerful, including me, but we knew we were all headed to the guillotine.*'

During the few months of cohabiting, Carla reported extreme stress at work. Her obsessional thoughts returned and now had a focus: she would imagine her lack of responsibility, such as forgetting material at the office, would lead to catastrophic consequences. She would be fired and be unable to get another job because of her negligence – fit punishment, we later thought, for her illicit living arrangements.

Interestingly, when Carla and her boyfriend were making plans to get married, none of her usual symptoms emerged – a happy surprise to both of us. They had a small wedding in a restaurant her parents frequented. By now, Carla had a much better understanding of her separation/growing up issues. She knew that she had tried to be good for her father and had tried to make him happy. Since she was the only one at home most of the time, she had understood this to be her responsibility. We reduced the frequency of our sessions at her request, as Carla adjusted to life with her husband and her job. She was basically symptom-free during this time.

There was an increase in obsessional symptomatology, however, when they planned to buy a house; for example, Carla had to check the stove in her apartment several times before leaving, and even then, was sure she had burned the place down. This time the obsessional worry was understood partly as related to her plan to leave their student-like, cramped, living arrangements, and the conflicts she experienced about her right to move forward. (See Modell's 1965 article described in the previous chapter.) If Carla's apartment burned down, then of course, she would have to move.

Carla's first impulse in buying a house was to consider her parents' neighbourhood; however, her rationalizations about 'convenience' soon rang hollow to both of us, and she was able to see that such an action would have afforded her the sense that she had made the next step in her separation easier for all of them. She did not particularly like the neighbourhood, however, and after some time and continued analysis of her motivations, she was able, with her partner, to find a property they both loved, in a different part of the city. Carla brought pictures to her session, saying she did not feel she deserved this beautiful house, needing my permission and unfettered encouragement. At this point, she was experiencing only mild symptomatology – perhaps because her parents had a financial share in the purchase and therefore were an integral part of this step. This may have provided them with a softer landing and mitigated the pain of their daughter's final leave-taking. The risk, of course, with financially stable parents, is that this kind of support may be a way of hanging on and of ensuring inclusion in their adult children's lives.

As our work together progressed, Carla had allowed herself to become more and more aware of how her particular family experience had influenced her difficulty in separating, and to begin to be aware of her own need for her inconsistent mother. Some months after the house purchase, Carla phoned me, sobbing. 'I think I'd better come in right away. I'm pregnant.' As we talked on the telephone, Carla said she had been happy for about 'five minutes' when she found out the news, and then had become frightened. She had not slept, and her obsessional thoughts were clamouring for recognition. She had immediately gone onto the Internet to find out how late one could terminate a pregnancy. Her reaction was even more confusing to her since she and her husband had planned to have a family. She had called me before telling her parents. I advised her to tell them before her session.

'How'd it go?' I asked.

'I couldn't stop crying,' she said. 'My father thought I was going to tell them I had cancer.'

'Well, what a relief that must have been, then, when you told them.'

'I guess so,' she said.

I was deep in thought about how difficult these developmental steps still were for her, and wondering if she felt she had gone 'too far' this time, by taking such an obvious separation step, when she said, 'But I thought I knew what you would say.'

'What?' I asked.

'That I felt that way and put it that way for my father, so he wouldn't think I was too happy to start a family of my own.'

Instead of cringing in horror at hearing this naked exposure of my formerly imagined opaque theory, I smiled to myself in smug satisfaction – for that session, at least – and congratulated Carla on this interpretation. And sure enough, as her anxiety lessened, Carla, though still somewhat fearful, began to enjoy her pregnancy.

There are three more parts to this story – one being Carla's husband, Ted, whose family background was very different from hers, and who acted as a reality check on many occasions when she was sure she was doing something very wrong. As will be described in the next chapter, marriage or long-term partnership can often serve as a catalyst for separation from one's family of origin. Another part was our understanding of the facilitative part of Carla's parents' role in this situation. Her mother, the victim of unconscious guilt about her earlier absence during Carla's growing up, idealized Carla, respected the treatment, and tried to do whatever she could to help, consciously pushing against her own avoidant tendencies – although it could be mentioned here that she had planned to attend a professional conference out of town on the date that Carla was due to give birth. Her father, who had provided a loving, although complicated presence in her early years, did well, in the end, by surviving Carla's separation and individuation in relatively good mental and physical health.

Another side note: during the time immediately after Carla moved in with her boyfriend, her father had begun to experience serious problems with his vision, which, of course, had affected his mood, complicating the situation. Had he been blinded by her leaving, or did he just not want to witness his daughter becoming an adult woman? In the tradition of 'sometimes a cigar…,' it turned out, much to our relief, that he was diagnosed with cataracts; after his surgery, his mood improved greatly and he began to take pleasure in the idea of a grandchild.

Her parents' marriage was the third crucial factor, as is often the case with these patients. The feeling that Carla was responsible for the care of her father was clearly implied by her mother's absence. Carla enjoyed his company when he wasn't drinking, but she could sense his need for her and his loneliness and isolation when she was not around, which had led to a limited social life in her teens and early twenties. Although her parents' marriage survived Carla's growth, we understood that their lack of intimacy had been a significant contributor to Carla's inability to leave home. Children who sense that they are the glue for the family demonstrate the burden of too much power in the manifestation of defensive symptomatology, including an inability to move forward because of the threat of a realized Oedipal victory, or a narcissistic over-investment in their own self-importance, which they know, unconsciously, will crumble and reveal them as imposters. In this case, neither parent became ill or depressed, or died. Despite his earlier behaviour, Carla's father was able to conquer the narcissistic injury of her leaving with another man, and to let himself be included with the new couple in a helpful way.

In the treatment, Carla established a working alliance fairly quickly. Despite her mother's frequent absences and her father's alcoholism, she had a secure attachment to both, as they had made their care and concern for her obvious; and this was transferred to me. She trusted me when I informed her that, although she was 18 years of age when we first met, I would not report to her mother about what transpired between us. We did not start with an analytic treatment, as Carla was tentatively on her way out and my sense was that analysis, although it may have speeded up the eventual process, would have slowed her down at this critical point – and would have given her yet another older person to worry about abandoning. The whole of our therapy together spanned ten years, covering an important developmental period in Carla's life.

Carla managed to achieve a rapprochement resolution with both parents after the baby was born – with their participation. Her father was able to visit on occasion and, hearing the baby cry, was able to understand that someone else needed her, and to offer assistance. Her expectations of her father became more limited, but appropriate to his abilities. Her mother took one day per week off work to help with the baby, and therefore was able to be more present with Carla than she had been in the past. Carla, for her part, was able to enjoy these times with her mother.

As has been stated earlier, there is a strong temptation in these situations for the analyst to be the good parent. Therapy offered Carla the experience of a consistent and reliable object. Her father, who had established a mutual caretaking relationship with her, found it extremely difficult to see her grow up sexually because of his own unresolved Oedipal issues and his need to keep her as a child to avoid acting on unconscious fantasies of incest. The analyst could be the reliable mother as well as the father who encouraged her to grow in all ways.

Because of her past experience of good-enough parenting, Carla made use of me as a non-judgmental new object (albeit one with a theory in mind). Her achievements in object constancy, and her basic trust in others, which benefited the positive transference, led her to keep trying at each stage she encountered. My developing empathic sense of when to move in and when to move out allowed Carla to have the unique experience of being with someone who followed her own time and pacing, as much as possible, more or less freed from worrying about, or caring for, someone else. Fortunately, we both had the luxury of time as these developmental stages were evolving in the therapeutic process.

## Clinical vignette 2.2

Lily, a 41-year-old professional, presented with symptoms of depression and extreme panic attacks that prevented her from attending social events and travelling, particularly by airplane – which she described as 'too fast'. She felt her work was not affected by these symptoms; she absorbed herself in it and was not very good at having fun. 'Work is more fun than fun', she said.

### Parents' history in brief

Lily's mother was from a large, controlling family in a big city; she was the second-youngest of ten siblings. She described her own mother as 'perfect' and her childhood as 'wonderful'; however, it had become evident to Lily as she was growing up that her mother was quite envious of her own younger sister, who had always seemed to have more than she did – as a child, and then later as an adult by marrying a wealthy man. Her mother's father had died at home of a heart attack when Lily's mother was 12 years of age, a trauma from which she never recovered. Throughout her marriage, Lily's mother had remained in thrall to her family of origin, to whom her husband and her children could never measure up. She defended against her envy of her younger sister with a rigid, unconscious idealization, a defence that never cracked until her death when Lily was in her late forties. Because of her psychic fragility, Lily's mother was often extremely angry, critical, and punitive with her new family – particularly in regard to Lily, who represented her younger, advantaged, and hated sibling.

Lily's father's mother died when her father was five years of age, after which he and his brother were sent to live with their grandmother, as their own abusive father did not want to raise them. The cause of her paternal grandmother's untimely death was never known and could only be imagined. No one in the family spoke about it. Her father and his brother managed their university education on their own and later worked together as professionals. Like Carla's mother, Lily's father had little or no contact with his family of origin and was swept up in her mother's large family.

In contrast to Lily's mother, her father was described by her as a kind, gentle, and well-respected professional man. Although he was not physically demonstrative, he was empathic to Lily's thoughts and emotions and was always interested and supportive. He was the type of person family members and friends would talk to when they had a problem. Where Lily's father let her down was in his inability to limit her mother's emotionally abusive and rageful behaviour, thereby contributing to Lily's doubt about her own self-worth. During our time together, we understood her father's powerlessness as related to memories of his own abusive father, probably unconsciously triggered by the woman he married.

### Early treatment

In the first few months of treatment, Lily cried throughout our sessions, sinking into the couch and the calm and non-intrusive quality of the analysis that she had needed so badly for so long. As she began to talk, Lily's guilt – literally from infancy – became startlingly evident. Because Lily's mother often expressed her rage quite primitively, the assaults from childhood were quite obvious. She complained frequently that Lily's birth 'almost killed her', as she had been a big baby. When Lily was an adolescent, her mother once found her looking into a mirror. 'Do you think you're beautiful? You're not', she said. And she blamed Lily for many of her ongoing physical problems – including, as she aged into her eighties, her osteoporosis, which she saw as being a result of her pregnancy with Lily.

Lotterman (2003) describes an individual's guilt about being born and the debt one can have for the gift of life. 'A very powerful form of guilt stems from a sense of having damaged the life-giving parent with one's most basic needs' (p. 547). Following Modell (1965), Lotterman states that the guilt of being born is manifested in patients who ask whether they are entitled to the satisfactions of life; they are often absorbed by the question of whether what they want threatens the survival of others. 'I propose that there exists a particular form of preoedipal guilt that consists of guilt about simply existing at all. This guilt about existing is often associated with fantasies about birth, especially of having damaged the mother' (Lotterman, 2003, p. 562).

### Middle treatment

Lily reported that when she was reaching puberty, at age 12, her father went into a deep depression from which he never completely emerged. She stated that it was a reaction to the death of his older brother, upon whom he had relied since losing his mother. In her analysis, she understood that this painful loss had triggered his aborted grieving for an even more painful loss, the death of his mother when he was five years of age. We noticed how the coincidence of this event had become unconsciously linked with her own maturing into puberty. At that time, Lily determined that her role in the family must be to protect her 'sick' father from her angry mother, who became even more aggressive as her husband became less available – probably unconsciously anticipating another abandonment over which she had no control. Lily's attempt to survive in this family led to defensive splitting: good parent/bad parent. Her response to feeling hated by her mother as she was growing up was to hate her; each became a (willing) container for the other's hatred. After her father became depressed, she idealized him as the lost good object and identified with him in an effort to cure him and bring him back: they looked alike, they liked the same things, and they reacted similarly to life events. At the same time, Lily had worked consciously at dis-identifying with her mother, which contributed to the acrimony between them and hermetically sealed the connection to her father. His not attempting to pry this seal apart spoke to her silently of his agreement and of his need for her.

Lotterman states that most commonly these patients develop some form of masochistic solution to the problem of wanting a life. In Lily's case, it involved an early marriage to someone who could not give her what she needed ('I'll leave home but I won't enjoy it.'). As well, she was never able to become pregnant, despite many intrusive investigations and treatments, although she had really wanted children. The bargain was made. To quote Lotterman,

A variety of masochistic outcomes is possible. Primitive and frank self-destructive behaviors such as suicide attempts ... [happen]. However, there are more subtle forms of self-deprivation. Sabotaging success, alienating loved ones, and enduring psychosomatic illness are a few of the many possibilities. Identification with the suffering of others (such as an unhappy or ill parent) is another.

(Lotterman, 2003, p. 561)

There is more to this story: her early marriage took Lily to another city and so must have been unconsciously, or as Lily put it, 'sneakily', done to extricate her from her family. However, her guilt became unbearable as her father seemed to become even more depressed after she left, and soon was bedridden because of an ongoing congenital physical illness, the symptoms of which were difficult to distinguish from his depression. She had abandoned her father to the care of her angry mother. Like the male patient I described in the first chapter, she was certain he would die without her. Two years after her marriage and many anguished trips home on weekends, Lily's father died – not from a broken heart, as she had imagined/feared/wished, but from the congenital illness that had beset him in the previous ten years – and thus abandoned her to her mother. This unfortunate event had an even more tragic significance for Lily, as we saw in the analysis; it was taken as evidence that she (or at least her leaving) had killed her valued father.

In the cases of both Carla and Lily, these daughters felt closer to their fathers than their mothers, albeit in different ways. The fact that both fathers performed 'maternal' functions in the home – making meals, acting as the nurturing parent – increased the strength of the daughters' attachment to them. Lily felt hated by her mother; Carla felt loved by hers. Each pair of parents had significant, one might say, pathological, unresolved separation issues from their own family of origin, as can be seen from the brief histories provided here. In Lily's case, both her parents had traumatic losses of one parent (their 'favourite') at a young age – her mother, at age 12, when her father died; her father, at age five, when his mother died. In Carla's case, her mother had been abandoned by her father at a young age, but she had taken the (proactive) step of leaving her remaining family; Carla's father was still involved with his family of origin, as was Lily's mother. The traumatic losses experienced by these parents contributed powerfully to their actions with their own children.

Lily's therapy was predictably more complicated than Carla's. As described earlier, she had been suffering from panic attacks, phobias concerning travel, even on the subway, and an inability to go into stores and restaurants for several years, before entering treatment. As we talked, we began to understand that the nature of her symptoms interfered significantly with her moving forward in adult life. The travel phobia (she had her first plane ride on her honeymoon) was seen as ensuring that she would not leave, and, like the patient mentioned in the first chapter whose parents both died close in time to her marriage, that she would not enjoy herself. The easing of those symptoms had to be addressed early on, for they were as painful and debilitating as they were satisfying and protective.

In Lily's situation, I was her second (female) analyst. Her first attempt at analysis had failed because the analyst could not endure the hatred that became evident as the maternal transference took hold. Although this was not articulated, I could sense it almost immediately. Being determined to be the good mother had gotten her first analyst into trouble. When a powerful emotion such as this – which is experienced as so negative and damning of the patient's character – is felt so completely, then it must eventually take centre stage. I found myself using the word *hate* before Lily did – confidently and frequently – in an attempt to normalize and allow for its expression: I had to be careful to let Lily hate me. If she had not been able to experience this, the analysis would have sputtered and stalled, as had happened in her previous analysis.

During the treatment, Lily's use of splitting became an increasing focus. All the splits seemed to be derivative of the original 'mother = bad' and 'father = good' compromise formation. As we tried to understand her experience and analyse the splits, Lily saw quite clearly her attempts to defend against feeling unloved by her mother, and therefore unlovable by anyone. She remembered being taken to see *The Wizard of Oz* as a young child and being so terrified by the Wicked Witch of the West that she cried and asked to go home. Lily also feared her own aggression towards her mother. By the time she was able to express her hatred in the treatment, Lily was also able to understand the 'as if'-ness of the transference and to marvel at the depth of what she had been feeling inside. Lily's use of splitting had given her a map to tread over the mines in the family. Only much later was she able to tentatively see her mother as the energetic and 'fun' person in the family, and her father as a bit 'stodgy'; also, she was able to understand how her father's undemonstrativeness partially contributed to her mother's frustration and rage. As she worked this through, Lily ventured to say that her mother, although limited in her own growth, was not a monster, and that her father, though wise and silent, had let her down by not actively encouraging her growth. Although Lily understood that her mother's emotionality frightened her father because of his very early experience of his own father's rage, she wished that he could have stood up to her mother, thereby protecting his own children from being in the line of fire as he must once have been. Thus, understanding more about her parents' histories was helpful in moderating the effect connected to the splitting.

To defend against her experience of not mattering in her family, Lily had burdened herself with the omnipotent fantasy that it was her responsibility to make her unhappy mother happy, and her sick and depressed father well. She needed help to face her feelings of being invisible in her family. Having been deprived of mirroring in her post-puberty life (after her father became ill), Lily thrived on being encouraged in the analysis to be all that she could be. Interpretations centred on an understanding of her own aggression could not be incorporated until later in the treatment. Lily had to know and analyse her feelings of being unlovable. And she had to forgive herself. Only then could she understand her mother, the catalyst for her hatred, and her father, the basis for her idealizing defence against anger and disappointment. The treatment continued until after the death of Lily's mother. Some years after her mother died, a part of the rapprochement crisis was resolved as Lily began to experience intense grief and to miss her mother very much. This was a very moving experience for both of us.

Comparing the stories of Carla and Lily – setting aside many significant details and many hours of therapy – one might speculate that Carla's superior survival depended on: first, her having had a loving, good-enough mother, who was not angry at her daughter, but was able to be encouraging when she was with her, and secondly, Carla's father surviving her leaving home. Although Carla imagined she had caused her father great emotional pain, she knew she had not killed him. Also, in Carla's case, the separation from her father was gradual – leaving home for school twice – and then returning to marry and live in the same city. In Lily's case, she lived at home during university – any attempts at leaving having been thwarted by her mother, who seemed to relish voicing the negative opinions of both parents. When she did leave, and moved directly out of town, the impact on her parents was more evident, and the guilt aroused in Lily, now very conscious, was monumental. In terms of Lotterman's masochistic solutions, we could partially understand Lily's inability to have a child as unconsciously spiteful. Once she married, her mother repeatedly expressed her need for Lily to have a child – interesting, in the light of her death-defying description of her own birthing experience. Thus Lily had the opportunity to express her hatred by withholding. Carla managed to have a baby, albeit with initial psychological difficulty.

In both cases, these daughters felt they had been given a 'duty' to their parents – unstated, of course, and therefore more powerful – to take care of one of them, because the other was unable to. As I have found in many cases of this kind, the parents had significant difficulty in their marriages: they were not close, they did not meet each other's needs, perhaps they did not even want to be together, but they were unable to end the marriage. And one of the offspring – the designated caretaker – picks up the job of keeping everything together and filling in with the needier parent.

Lily was haunted by hatred. Therefore, her potential for destructiveness (of her parents, particularly her mother, even though it was actually her father who was holding onto her) meant she could not enjoy the fruits of separate adulthood. Lotterman states,

> Since the child has no independent yardstick by which to measure the goodness of his love, he is vulnerable to the capriciousness of his mother's motives. In effect, his fate depends on her decency. By decency, I mean the responsibility based on devotion and love to see to it that the child grows to be as happy, strong, and free as possible.
>
> (Lotterman, 2003, p. 564)

Later attachment research has shown that adults' (parents') attachment styles are highly predictive of their children's attachment styles.

Lily developed a defensive false self (Winnicott, 1960) to cope with her mother's hostility and with what she perceived of as her father's needs. Her aggressive and destructive urges were covered by a 'sweetness' and compliance that often made us quite sad as she described it. Everyone liked Lily because she was so 'nice'; however, her unconscious attempt to show her mother how nice she was and thereby that she should love her, only made their relationship worse. Lily was generous and giving (father) and never angry (mother) – on the outside. However, inside, she 'knew' her mother was right – that she was rotten, jealous, and sneaky. This false self, which had seemed to serve her well until she came for treatment, became unbearable during her analysis, and she began to lash out at friends, and the analyst, mostly in sarcastic witticisms – which sometimes made us both laugh, as she had an excellent sense of humour. Her reaction formation, as seen in her false self, served as a defence against her deep murderous rage. Carla, who had been encouraged to be her real self during her childhood, and whose real self was genuinely valued by both parents, used denial in that part of her relation to her father where she was expected to take care of him – which she acknowledged in treatment she hated doing, and which interfered with her wished-for admiration of him.

Lily also had to understand that she was experiencing the effects of her mother's envy – although not consciously. In fact, she had never heard of parents envying their children and was surprised to hear that they could. Her mother's unprotected envy, meant for her younger sister, was displaced unmetabolized onto her daughter.

The work of Melanie Klein on envy is relevant here, as is the work of Clifford Scott (2013), who states that where there is envy, it must be dealt with before anything else is possible. Klein, of course, saw envy as operating from the beginning of life (oral-sadistic). She defines envy as,

> the angry feeling that another person possesses and enjoys something desirable, the envious impulse being to take it away or to spoil it. Moreover, envy implies the subject's relation to one person only and goes back to the exclusive relation with the mother.
>
> (Klein, 1975, p. 180)

In Lily's case, envy seemed to play an important role in both directions. In Klein's thinking, very early on, Lily may have been envious of her mother's breast (not literally, as she was bottle fed); in Oedipal time, she was envious of her mother for having her desired father; later in life, she was envious of her mother for having been able to have children. However, the most destructive form of the mutual envy seemed to be in its expression of her mother's envy of her – of her relationship with her father, of her youth and beauty, of her potential capacity for a better life. Her mother's defensive tendency to project her feelings of self-hatred onto her daughter, thereby declaring her worthless, did not function well enough to preclude her feelings of envy from being aroused, probably because of the reality of her daughter, which she could not completely deny.

The unconscious erotic fuelling of the intense hatred on both sides triggered unconscious homosexual desires, which were brought to the surface in the analysis. As she described life at home, Lily remembered her mother wearing transparent nightgowns, without a robe, and sprinkling her speech with provocative sexual terms, most of which indicated disgust, giving her children too clear a glimpse into her unmet sexual needs. Before her death, Lily's mother had a stroke that left her paralyzed and unable to speak; for the first time, Lily saw her smile at her warmly when she visited – a smile she had longed for all her life.

As was mentioned earlier, Lily managed a satisfying intrapsychic separation from her mother and a more-or-less complete resolution of the rapprochement crisis, only some years after her mother's death. Until then, the acrimonious relationship between them changed only slightly. We could hypothesize that, although separation can be achieved with 'only one hand clapping', Lily's undernourished masochistic personality, fed by the spring of her mother's sadism from birth, endured too great an impact.

Carla's satisfying resolution with both her parents emanated from having obtained good-enough resources from each of them early on, and from feeling valued by both, which created ego strength and resilience, and a fairly accurate sense of herself. Therefore, less extreme defences sufficed in her situation, at least for most developmental hurdles. Carla's parents, separately, were willing to let go of their daughter in order to keep her. Carla's own acceptance of their limitations – in other words, her ability to de-idealize and forgive them – allowed her to enjoy what they were able to give.

Darren Aronofsky's film *Black Swan* is the story of Nina (played by Natalie Portman), a young ballet dancer who is kept childlike by Erica, an envious and engulfing 'mommy' (played by Barbara Hershey). Hershey gives a chilling depiction of a has-been dancer, who, she tells us, gave up her career to have her beautiful daughter. She feels intense hatred of her, disguised only thinly by a cloying sweetness. Erica is inappropriately intrusive, emotionally and physically, and is always in her daughter's mind as her daughter tries to pursue her own career. Even when Nina, in a desperate attempt to grow up, experiments with masturbation in her pink room surrounded by her stuffed animals, she sees a vision of her mother just as she is reaching orgasm. Afterward, she shoves her stuffed animals into the incinerator.

The dance scenes in this film are beautiful, yet this is, in essence, a horror movie. As the male dance director takes over Erica's role with her, Nina starts to bleed, and we are given a grisly preview of the psychotic state that is to come. It is not clear whether Nina is injuring herself or is imagining all this blood. The self-flagellation of the ballet shoes and other deprivations speak to Nina's masochistic underbelly. She imagines a lesbian encounter with a fellow dancer – not surprisingly, considering her mother's constant caressing and assumed ownership of her body, which must have stirred forbidden urges, in addition to her narcissistic attraction to someone who looked like her. Just as Nina, as a dancer, has earlier replaced her mother, who yearns to be young and to dance again, she later replaces an older female dancer in the company, who can hate her openly, and who jumps in front of a car, as a result of losing the competition with Nina, almost killing herself. The cost of separation and of succeeding in one's passion, above all others, is high, and in the end, Nina pays the ultimate price.

## Clinical vignette 2.3

Ben, a 38-year-old professional, was referred to me by his mother, concerned that he was very anxious at work. Ben was a modern Orthodox Jew, who spent every weekend at his parents' home, even though he had a separate place of residence, invoking his religious affiliation as his reason for his frequent, prolonged visits. As he told me, he wanted to spend Friday evenings and Saturdays with them, partly because their home was close to the synagogue, and partly because he felt they needed him for this weekly observance. Also, his father was ailing – not fatally – and Ben was able to help him sort out his business affairs on Sundays. Ben's complaint when he came for treatment was anxiety at work, and the knowledge that he could never be as successful as his father (let alone surpass him). He had no social life and had never dated, stating that there was plenty of time for that later. His synagogue activities took up whatever spare time he had during the week and seemed to involve administrative duties rather than social functions.

When I questioned him, as gently as possible, about his weekends, Ben became immediately defensive. He did not see his actions as unusual and felt that I must not understand his commitment to his faith. His younger sister had managed to marry, moving out of town, but that left him to care for his ageing parents. Besides, as he explained to me, since his father was having trouble walking, he had to accompany his mother to social events related to their family's charitable donations, and to help her with the activities of daily living that she could not manage on her own.

Unfortunately, as Ben began to realize the complexity of his situation, he became increasingly resistant to the treatment. As his father, who had been the powerful head of the family, aged and became weaker, the possibility of actually surpassing him was greater, thereby unleashing early unconscious castration fears and the possibility of a realized fantasied Oedipal victory. His initial presentation of difficulties at work could now be understood, at least partially, in this light. Also, Ben began to be aware of his felt debt to his parents, his resentment of feeling forced to repay it, and his own strangulating fear of a lonely life without them. Was there really any way that he might actually be able to have a life separate from his parents without 'murder'? All of this he saw as very much in opposition to his religious beliefs, and that he was the worst of sons to possibly have these kinds of thoughts in his unconscious. He convinced himself that he should not go any further, that his work problems had been solved, and he left treatment after one year. Rapprochement, where he could enjoy the company of his (living) parents on his own terms, which might be different from theirs, was not a concept he could stay in treatment long enough to imagine.

### Clinical vignette 2.4

In another brief example, Diana, a 50-year-old mild-mannered artist, was seen in therapy for several years because she was having phobic anxiety about performing in her artistic job. She described herself as a generally anxious person who had trouble accomplishing anything and was plagued by negative thoughts about herself. Her father, a well-known artist in her area, had high expectations for her but was not at all tuned in to the kind of support she would have needed to excel, which made us suspicious of his fear of her talent. The not-so-hidden message to her was: I expect you to do fairly well, but not as well as I have done. Diana's mother was a complaining, depressed woman who often embarrassed Diana in public with her loud voice. She had a habit of visiting Diana when she was trapped at home with young children and confiding her complaints about her unhappy life, including her marriage. During these visits, Diana had tried to sympathize with her mother, knowing that she was the only one who listened. Even after Diana's children were grown, her mother continued to come around, and on a recent visit, told her the details of her relationship with her first boyfriend who had caused her to lose her virginity – which Diana related to me in therapy. We understood from her dream following this visit that this time her mother had gone too far: *My sister and I were in an amusement park on a ride that was kept going around because of the gunshots. I realized that I was entrusted with a severed head in a bag. I don't know why.*

The mild-mannered Diana was shocked at the degree of violence implied in the dream. Her associations led her to realize how much her mother was always in her head, and also that the negative thoughts about herself with which she was plagued were partly composed of her mother's own self-loathing, projected onto her, which she had previously denied. After years of this unquestioned behaviour, Diana was able to explore her archaic need to keep her mother close, and to begin to establish clear boundaries with her.

Both parents contributed to Diana's inability to pursue her chosen career, and ensured that she would not shine. Her father's lack of encouragement of her obvious talent from a young age, when she idealized him, and her mother's time-consuming use of her to complain to, made Diana feel that it was right that she, unlike her older sister who was in business, should be satisfied with less in life. (Diana makes another appearance in the chapter on siblings (Chapter 4), as does Lily.)

Much of the therapeutic work with these patients involves taking two important directions, sometimes at the same time: (1) analysis of the defences, often devised very early in life, that are based on perceived life-and-death survival experiences; and (2) provision of an alternative caring, interested, and invested object, who encourages individuation and can be left without disaster (see Chapter 5 on termination).

The patients who have been described above made use of their often maladaptive defences when they saw no other way out – splitting, denial, creation of a false self, and reaction formation, along with repression. These defences can be gently yet persistently confronted in analysis by involving the patient in observing the damage these formerly 'adaptive' ways of coping does in their contemporary life, and how they counteract their ability to enjoy the separate, mature, adult life to which they are entitled. 'Most defenses operate unconsciously. Because they involve organized, structured processes we think of defenses as residing in the unconscious part of the ego' (Fernando, 2009, p. 15). In analysing patients' defences and their need for them, it is imperative that the wish to separate – to harm, and even to kill – be brought into the light of adult day and subjected to robust examination; in other words, uncovering the intense ambivalence with which these patients are burdened – the ambivalence that underlies the stalled growth – is the only way out.

As we know, providing an alternative 'good' object may be even trickier than analysing defences, especially with patients like Lily, who use splitting. The temptation for the analyst to align with the 'good' parent soon becomes obvious. The work of analysis then involves courage on both parts: for the analysand, to take the risk of projecting the bad object onto the analyst, and for the analyst, to allow it and even encourage it. To receive the negative projections can be surprisingly difficult, and in some cases, intolerable. The patient also must have the courage to let themselves take stock of the contributions of both the good and the bad parent when subjecting themselves to analysing the split. This may result in a realization that one has been 'wrong' all along, carrying an 'inaccurate' internal representation since childhood. As good-enough parents do, we also have to move in and out at the 'right' times, giving, the 'gentle push' referred to earlier, but always remaining in tune with our patients' ambivalence: the need to abandon us and the fear of being abandoned. In our desire to save our patients from the fate brought about by insensitive, narcissistic, clinging, and sometimes hostile parents, and in our fervent wish for their independence and growth, we may push too hard or too fast, thereby skidding over the deeper traumas that have brought them to this impasse. Sandler's (1976) article on role-responsiveness warns us that the analyst can be caught in the patient's need to rush or their desire to linger. The counter-transference issues that arise here highlight the analyst's personal experiences in the area of separation–individuation. This topic will be discussed further in Chapter 5, on termination.

## Quotable quotes

Before ending this chapter, I wanted to offer a few quotes from patients I have seen in recent years that explain how my interest in this area was ignited. In these examples, the ages and professions are accurate.

Joanne, 53, lawyer, when her mother was dying: *'It's like I'm attached to an umbilical bungee cord – and I have been all my life. I'm dying along with my mother. I can't be happy unless she's happy.'*

Steve, 31, performer: *'My mother and I breathe the same oxygen.'*

Elsa, 47, executive hire: *'My mother gave me a* 101 Dalmatians *outfit for my 30th birthday. I never even liked* 101 Dalmatians*! What was she trying to do?'*

Dan, 30, PhD in computer science: *'I haven't gone to the gym in the years since my father had a stroke. It feels like it's me – like I've been injured.'*

Edna, 52, international aid consultant: *'I feel like I owe my parents something – like money, like I should write them a cheque.'*

Barbara, 50, psychologist, forced, because of her marriage, to live and have her children in a different city from her parents, but longing to go home again: *'It's like a transplant that didn't take.'*

*Quad erat demonstrandum.*

## References

Bergman, A. and I. Harpaz-Rotem (2004). Revisiting rapprochement in the light of contemporary developmental theories. *Journal of the American Psychoanalytic Association, 52*(2), 556–570.

Klein, M. (1975). *Envy and gratitude and other works 1946–1963.* M. M. R. Kahn (Ed.), International Psycho-Analytical Library, 104, 1–346. London: Hogarth Press and the Institute of Psycho-Analysis.

Lotterman, A. C. (2003). Guilt about being born and debt concerning the gift of life. *Journal of the American Psychoanalytic Association, 51*, 547–578.

Modell, A. H. (1965). On having the right to a life: An aspect of the superego's development. *International Journal of Psychoanalysis, 46*, 323–331.

Sandler, J. (1976). Countertransference and role-responsiveness. *International Review of Psychoanalysis, 3*, 43–47.

Scott, C. (2013). *Overcoming self-envy and learning to love the unconscious.* Paper read posthumously at the Canadian Psychoanalytic Society meeting, June 2013.

Winnicott, D. W. (1960). The theory of the parent–infant relationship. *International Journal of Psychoanalysis, 41*, 585–595.

# Chapter 3

# Oedipal victor or victim
## Couples

*Note: Parts of this chapter have been revised from my earlier publication:* Usher, S. F. (2015). *Hope and hopelessness in the couple relationship. In S. Akhtar and M. K. O'Neil (Eds.),* Hopelessness: Developmental, cultural, and clinical realms *(pp.165–180), with the permission of the publisher, Karnac.*

The lyrics of the Frank Sinatra love song, 'Fly Me to Moon', speak to the feeling/hope that true love can take us into the stratosphere. As mentioned in the last chapter, a relationship can often serve as a catalyst for leaving home – maybe not in travelling as far away as those wishful lyrics imply, but help in leaving nevertheless. Couples I have seen in their twenties, thirties and forties often seem still to be in what Mahler referred to as the practising sub-phase together – encountering quite serious issues of separation from their parents, sometimes more evident in one partner than the other. Forming the partnership – moving in together, or getting married – may have constituted a more or less sanctioned way out, one of many attempts to leave depressed, ill, controlling, overly 'loving' or abusive parents. It is a relief at first to establish a new home – sometimes far away geographically – and even a new family. For some individuals, marrying outside their religion or interracially feels or looks like a significant individuation, as mentioned in the last chapter. In an attempt to facilitate women's independence, the Women's Liberation Movement of the 1970s encouraged women to take a stand about retaining their surnames when they marry. Keeping the family/father's name was seen as a sign of independence from the husband; however, this practice can actually tie women back to their family of origin and to their childhood, and can be seen as a way of not leaving home. Taking these external factors into account, when couples decide to marry, unless internal issues of separation have been or are being worked through, the relationship may flounder – and sometimes fail.

Although couples, unlike individuals, seldom come for therapy explicitly for personal growth, one or both partners may unknowingly be in the throes of separation difficulties – often demonstrating excessive concern about keeping parents happy, financially secure or mediating a parent's depression. For couples, as well as for individuals, not only do the parents' own separation achievements, or lack thereof, matter, but so does the state of the parents' marriage. In addition to creating concern for the offspring, the parents' marriage can provide a role model of a mature – or immature – adult relationship. Perhaps one could say that the ideal marriage has survived the differentiation, practising and rapprochement crisis sub-phases of the individual partners separately and together, allowing them to have firm boundaries in who they are.

Couples therapy provides a fascinating look into the dynamics of intimate object relationships, often in terms of difficulties in separation. There are times in the treatment when the office feels very crowded, as one or the other partner's parents – or, indeed, both – are in the room with us, and as each partner's relationship with them is highlighted in a unique way, often quite differently from how we see it in individual work.

> As psychoanalytic understanding has deepened and explored yet earlier processes of interaction, so it has aided attempts to deepen understanding of the nature of the couple relationship. The many and complex fears and phantasies, joys and pleasures of earliest object relationships will be reactivated in the interaction between partners, as well as in their joint relationship to the environment they live in.
>
> (Ruszczynski, 1993, p. 20)

Classical theory, particularly our understanding of the impact of the Oedipal phase, is relevant in the formulation and treatment of problems couples present. Karen Horney (1967) was one of the few early analytic writers to discuss the effects of early development, mainly Oedipal love experiences, on individuals' later relationships. She writes that the problem for males who 'recoil' from the forbidding female is the notion of the saintliness of women, which interferes with sexual desires for the wife. She goes on to say that divorce is less related to 'the annoying qualities of the partner, and much more [to] the unresolved conflicts we bring into the marriage from our own development' (p. 131).

In terms of object relations theories, the contribution of Margaret Mahler has been discussed and will continue to be mentioned. Melanie Klein's thoughts about envy can be applied in understanding the relationship between the partners, and in their real or imagined relationship with one or both parents. Klein's concept of projective identification is an extremely useful way of thinking about the internal workings of couple relationships. Unconscious partner choice, according to Klein, is made on the basis of the other's responsiveness to projected aspects of the self – a kind of mutual projective identification society (Usher, 2008). Projective identification can be used by one partner to blame the other for an inability to separate from a difficult parent. Or it may be used as a cover for one partner's envy of the other's smoother relationship with the family of origin.

W.R.D. Fairbairn (1963) thought that the problems that arise within an adult relationship were due to a breakdown of the caring component in the earlier mother–child relationship, rather than to individual internal conflict. Reminding us of the adhesiveness of the libido, he observed and was struck by how abused children were intensely attached and loyal to their parent(s). Applying his theory to the thesis of this book, it becomes more evident that troubled parents are harder to leave. (For a more complete explication of how psychoanalytic theory can be applied to work with couples, see Usher, 2008.)

Cantor (1982) states that many divorces result from a couple's working through the task of separation–individuation at an adult level – not before. 'In a marriage, through the gratification of sexual desires, each partner introjects the other as a gratifier of needs and becomes a part of the self-system of the other' (p. 308). Interestingly, Cantor reminds us that historically, men differentiated as they developed increasing ego strength in their work, and in the past, marriages may have dissolved because men outgrew their wives. Even at the time she wrote, the developmental thrust in women was evident. 'Like the infant, their first steps toward differentiation are tentative. They move out slowly, taking a course or working part-time. The differentiation phase is overlapped by a practicing period (during which the wife returns home periodically)' (p. 309). Mahler states that in certain toddlers – and we can say in certain adults – the readiness to separate produces a feeling of panic, as has been referred to earlier. With adults, the intense interaction with parents, developed over many years, may make it difficult to tease out the contributing factors.

Whether a relationship can survive the separation–individuation crisis of one partner when the other partner is more or less already on the way, becomes a compelling challenge. This is complicated because, as Fairbairn and the other object relations scholars have taught us, each partner in the couple will have a unique need for attachment, connectedness and bonding. These needs may be different; some may be complementary – in a healthy or a pathological way – in the partners. Still, in order to connect with a new significant other in a truly intimate manner, one must have achieved a certain degree of separation from one's earlier objects, and it is the hope of those of us who treat couples that Mahler's stages – particularly her third (rapprochement) and fourth (consolidation of individuality) – will be experienced compatibly, eventually, by the couples we treat.

As it happens, the cases portrayed here are well-educated, heterosexual couples. These hurdles also occur in same-sex and transgendered couples, and in couples who are not professionally educated.

## Clinical vignette 3.1

Pamela and Tom, professionals in their early forties, came for therapy because Tom was certain he had no sexual feelings for his partner and felt their ten-year relationship was over.

### Family history in brief

Tom's parents, both blue-collar workers, lived in a small town close to the city, where they both worked for an auto company. Tom had experienced their behaviour as embarrassing when he was growing up. They both smoked and drank too much, walked around the house completely naked, and used the washroom with the door open. Tom's mother was described as needy and unable to cope on her own. Tom's older brother had married a woman who encouraged their move to New Zealand. His brother's move was a significant loss for Tom and left him with the care of their ageing parents.

Pamela's parents both immigrated to Canada from China with their families as adolescents. Neither parent had the opportunity to attend university. Pamela's mother was the dominant of the two, making all the decisions for the family. She had very high hopes for her daughter, seeing her as brighter than her son, Pamela's older brother, whom she devalued, as she did her husband. Even though she encouraged Pamela to do well in university and to pursue graduate work, so that she would not have to rely on a man, she was also extremely critical of her. During Pamela's latency years, her mother had left for long periods of time. Pamela explained that she was interested in bowling and had joined a league that travelled. The bowling metaphor was well used as the therapy went on.

### Early treatment

Tom and Pamela were referred for couple's therapy by Tom's family doctor. Tom had been experiencing increased stress and was on the verge of depression. In our beginning sessions, Tom cried a lot, saying that he wished he could feel attracted to Pamela, whom he loved very much. Pamela sat in silence, listening, speaking only occasionally to add observations and clarifications based on what Tom had been expressing.

When Tom and Pamela were first married, Tom's parents, who lived about an hour away, expected the couple to visit them frequently, which they often did on weekends. About two years into their relationship, Tom's father died suddenly, and the health of his mother, for whom he had always been the 'good son', began to deteriorate rapidly, her diabetes worsening as a result of her increased smoking and drinking. Pamela and Tom were then expected to visit every second weekend without fail, and now to stay overnight in his mother's chaotic home. As she became increasingly ill, Tom's mother refused to hire help; therefore, the couple were obliged to do the heavy care, including toileting, themselves. Pamela, who had felt she could never please her own mother, was happy that someone seemed to appreciate her. Tom acknowledged that he had always known that he would never marry anyone who could not get along with his mother, even though she was difficult and demanding.

As time went on, Tom and Pamela were becoming more like siblings than like partners, and their sex life, never very active after their marriage, was more and more infrequent – in a manner that seemed agreeable to both. When Tom's mother finally died, they were in their late thirties. As they were no longer preoccupied with travelling to Tom's mother's house, this seemed to them to be a good time to think about having a child. Ovulation thermometer in hand, they set about trying to have intercourse at the 'right' time. Tom found sex on demand even worse than no sex. They ultimately managed to conceive and had a baby girl. However, both felt totally unequipped to care for an infant. Tom's response to this new anxiety was to work harder, spending many evening hours at his company, leaving Pamela alone with the baby.

Pamela's parents rushed to the rescue. Her mother, delighted with the opportunity to make up for her own negligent parenting (see 'Family history in brief', above), immediately took over much of the baby's care. I could say here that Pamela's father moved in, and I would not be using metaphor. He established himself in their guest room, to help with the baby during the night. Pamela, seeing this as an opportunity to please her parents, welcomed them into her home. I think of this as the 'bait-and-switch' technique, wherein the grandparents, who want to hang onto their child, are given the grandchild instead, freeing up the baby's mother or father to separate from them. It is similar to offering a baby an attractive toy in order to be able to remove a dangerous or otherwise unacceptable object from their grasp.

This tactic also relieved Pamela of her anxiety with the baby, and of any need for intimacy – particularly sexual intimacy – with Tom. Tom became angrier, feeling increasingly left out of the family, and saw himself as needed only for the money he brought home. This led to more late nights at the office, and so it went on. As well, instead of experiencing the deep sadness he expected after the death of his mother, Tom began to act out his grief. He became heavily involved with a group of colleagues at work, one of whom was a flirtatious, attractive woman, and he stayed out until the early morning hours. Since he felt unwanted and unneeded at home, this 'solution' seemed perfect.

In the beginning of their treatment, we spent many hours talking about their families of origin and how they had allowed them to intrude, not only in their sex life, but in their relationship as well. We revisited their lack of opportunity for sex and intimacy during their marriage thus far, and understood that neither of them had been ready (did not feel 'grown up' enough) for the kind of relationship they imagined that marriage entailed; both had been deeply affected by the lack of harmony in their parents' marriages. They were able to acknowledge that they had colluded with, or enabled, their parents' behaviour. After several months of therapy, Pamela asked her father to move out of their house and worked hard at keeping her parents at bay. Tom continued to express severe pain in our sessions, wishing he could feel something for Pamela that he did not feel. I referred him to individual therapy, where he was apparently able to express his deep sadness over the loss of his father, his mother, and now Pamela and their daughter – as he could not bring himself to feel sexual feelings for Pamela, and he did not want a marriage without sex.

### Middle treatment

As the therapy progressed, we worked together to interpret the effects of the intrusions on their relationship by the combination of parents on both sides who could not let their children grow up, and the 'children' who did not want to grow up. Both partners had seriously thought their first duty was to make their parents happy – and both completely agreed that meant their marriage was second. They became loving siblings on the surface and angry partners not too far beneath. When we talked about people marrying to get pulled out of the muck of their original families, Pamela said, almost proudly, 'I jumped right in; I got into it with them.' Tom responded, 'I needed that – I needed to make my parents happy.'

During the treatment, Tom acknowledged that he had actually been relieved when Pamela's parents had moved in with the baby, now assured that Pamela would not make demands on him. Also, he had never felt comfortable with infants; however, when the child started to grow, he found himself strongly attached to her and wanted another baby. Pamela's mother had advised her not to have another child, as her husband was never around, and when he was around, he was 'useless'. Pamela said that she would have wanted another child, but was 'fine' with her mother's advice.

There was a column in the newspaper when I was growing up called 'Can This Marriage Be Saved?', which I used to read with great curiosity. The answer in this case was, unfortunately, no. The therapy – with two intelligent and psychologically minded individuals who still cared deeply for each other – was too late. In a two-hour tearful session, after a year and a half of couples therapy, they made the decision to part. In this case, the partners were matched on difficulties with separation–individuation, although these difficulties were experienced in very different ways. Tom continued in his personal therapy. I referred Pamela to individual treatment after we terminated.

## Clinical vignette 3.2

Nate and Caroline, both successful professionals, also in their early forties, married with three children, were referred for couples therapy by Nate's individual therapist. Nate presented the problem: 'We both have tough mothers.' Caroline nodded her head vigorously in agreement. He continued, 'This is causing so much stress, it may be fatal to our marriage.'

### Family history in brief

Nate's parents met and married in the southern United States. His mother's father had been a Christian minister. The family was fairly conventional and financially comfortable. His father was the head of a large corporation, and his mother did not work outside the home. Nate had an older brother and a younger sister, both of whom were married, had children and lived not far from their parents. Nate was the only one who had moved away. Nate described his mother as domineering and tending to complain a great deal during his childhood. 'It was impossible for any of us to make her smile.'

Caroline's parents were both professionals living in Toronto. Her mother was from a very wealthy family. Caroline described her as having a 'huge, unpredictable temper'. Caroline's father had abandoned the family when Caroline was two years of age, after which she had very little contact with him. Being an only child, who had experienced the trauma of parental separation during her practising and rapprochement sub-phases, Caroline was very vulnerable to her mother's needs. Her mother forced the two of them into a sticky symbiotic unit, adopting a you-and-me-against-the-world attitude. Even so, she was often outrageously mean to Caroline and extremely critical. Caroline was trapped in an insecure attachment to this hyper-emotional, probably personality disordered, mother.

### Early treatment

Nate and Caroline had met while they were working in India; they had then lived together for two years in Europe, and then had moved back to Caroline's hometown to marry and have children.

Both felt that the relationship with their mothers, particularly with Caroline's mother, who lived in the same city, was problematic. Their method of dealing with Caroline's mother, until they entered treatment, had been to avoid her as much as possible; for example, they lied about their vacations so that her mother would not 'surprise' them by joining them, or cause them to feel guilty about not inviting her along. 'Every decision I have ever made has been with my mother in mind. I don't know my own mind,' Caroline said.

From the beginning of our work together, almost entire sessions were focused on Caroline's difficulties with what she perceived as an intrusive, demanding and controlling mother. Nate reported that he was actually excluded from conversations when Caroline's mother visited, and so he had the opportunity to observe their interaction. He could see how difficult it was for Caroline, but he felt helpless. When any command performance reared its head – such as Mother's Day, or a holiday, Caroline would collapse into panic and be unable to make decisions. Caroline's fear of her mother's rage became conflated with her own murderous rage, an internalization of her mother's projected hatred of her rejecting father. This led to significant unconscious guilt.

Although Nate's mother was quieter in her presentation, she made it clear that she thought that Caroline was overprotective of their children – a reaction to Caroline's not trusting her to be alone with the children on their visits. She also told Caroline that she was too lenient with the children in terms of discipline. Both Nate's parents, but particularly his mother, repeatedly reminded them that they did not visit enough. Nate had been brought up to honour and respect his parents and to not go against them. Therefore, he felt guilty about having moved away and not having visited his parents as much as they would have liked. Caroline's discomfort with them dictated the paucity of their visits in both directions; thus, the tension between Caroline and Nate grew. Although both partners described Nate's mother as extremely negative and dissatisfied with any plans they painstakingly made for their visits – often complaining of fatigue or physical illness – Nate continued to be very clear about needing to make these visits entertaining. He saw this situation as a conflict with Caroline that would 'never end'.

### Middle treatment

As we worked with both partners' 'mother issues' – in addition to their other difficulties – Nate began to change. Using both his individual therapy and the couples therapy, he came to realize that, in terms of his own family of origin, the 'right' thing for him to do was to stand up for Caroline, not his mother, particularly on issues concerning their children, and he began to develop the necessary resources to do this. Although he still respected his parents, he was able to see how much his mother's criticisms affected Caroline, and could let himself judge them as overstepping. This took some time, particularly impeded by his guilt over being the only 'child' not living in the United States, but he was able to stick to their new terms of frequency of visits in both directions, and to support Caroline and her wishes with the children over those of his mother. During our work, Nate gained an understanding of his mother as suffering from a lifelong depression for which he was not the catalyst. This discovery was extremely helpful in supporting him in his stance with Caroline and his mother, and in furthering his own efforts at separation. As Nate became more and more able to see the positive effect his changes had on Caroline, he was determined to allow himself to continue. Caroline, for her part, now feeling supported, made every attempt to make the previously dreaded visits with Nate's parents a better time for all of them.

At this point in the treatment, Nate emailed me a cartoon from the *New Yorker*:

The situation with Caroline and her mother reached a peak over a long holiday weekend, when Nate and Caroline and their children were visiting her mother at her country home. They had planned to have lunch one day during that weekend with their friends who lived nearby. Hearing about this lunch, Caroline's mother became enraged, and a physical fight ensued. We decided in our next session that Caroline would take a break from seeing or speaking to her mother. Her mother's response to Caroline's attempt to pull away was, 'This is just like a divorce', thereby revealing her unconscious need for Caroline as a spouse and life partner.

Caroline's part in this tortuous dilemma could not be fully dealt with in the couples therapy. Did she suspect that she was the cause of her parents' break-up (at age two), either because her father had loved her more than he had loved her 'crazy' mother, or because her father had hated her since she had been 'bad' in some way? Caroline became conscious of her fear that *she* would not survive without her mother who was so enmeshed in her life. Did this fear derive from this early loss? We knew that she believed it was her duty to look after her mother and never leave her, thereby not repeating the traumatic loss of her father for either of them.

After about a year of couples therapy, I referred Caroline for individual analytic work, while the couples therapy continued, and in this way I legitimized the problem and also set up the expectation that it could be resolved. Caroline had been sinking into her mother's psychopathology with no one to pull her out – no sibling, no father. It became her two therapists' and Nate's job to extricate her. I can still hear the sucking sound as she finally had the courage to allow herself to be withdrawn from the quicksand.

Through our work, the newly enlightened Nate had been able to understand Caroline's painful dilemma – a seemingly intractable desire to meet her mother's needs, her unconscious conviction that she needed her mother to survive, and her low self-esteem and lack of confidence that were the result of her mother's constant criticism, all of which were making it impossible for her to 'leave home'. If the climate in the couples therapy is effective, these observations can be understood by both partners, and thereby contribute to a quickening of the shifts for both.

After some time, Caroline and Nate were in this together and they both could feel it. Nate felt more valued by Caroline, as she no longer participated in conversations with her mother that excluded him. Not only could he be genuinely helpful in supporting Caroline's endeavours to free herself from the pathological enmeshment with her mother, but he could also provide Caroline with a mature, loving and healthy alternative.

For this couple, there were significant other-than-mother factors affecting their relationship, but as the emphasis here is on separation, I have focused on the factors related to it. In this example, the mothers of the partners had the most difficulty letting go: the adult child's enmeshment with both their earliest objects was the most difficult to moderate for both partners. In my experience, just as with any other form of abuse, there is often a secrecy about the extent of the enmeshment between the parent(s) and the child. When this is brought out into the open, the gig is up, so to speak – probably more dramatically evident in couples therapy because of the partner's presence.

Modell's (1965) concept of having the right to a life, described in Chapter 1, is paramount in a couple's having the right to a life together. In the above example, Caroline felt that in many ways she had a life: a husband, a professional life and three essentially problem-free children. But she still remained tied to an emotionally unpredictable mother. The difficulty of separating from a parent who won't let go depends on the ego strength of both the 'child' and the parent. One fuelled the other in this case. Because Nate had been provided with good-enough parenting growing up, he had the internal resources to push on to separation; his mother was also endowed enough to be able to let go – at least a little. Still, Nate managed to separate, even though his mother felt angry and abandoned. Of course, environmental factors, such as having a husband and two other children who lived nearby, undoubtedly helped his mother ease her hold on Nate and increased his feeling that she would survive. As Nate's attitude changed, the couple were able to spend more time with friends than parents on their subsequent visits to the United States; therefore Nate enjoyed seeing his parents more and Caroline tolerated the visits better. His mother, reassured that he did want to see her, resigned herself to spending less – but happier – time with them.

Aristotle, in a description written two and a half millennia ago (cited in Young-Bruehl, 2012), stated, 'The parent gives the child the greatest gifts, its existence, but also cherishment and education … and because the child receives, it owes the parent honor and helpfulness' (p. 1). Young-Bruehl goes on to say, 'People as individuals and in societies mistreat children in order to fulfill certain needs through them, to project internal conflicts and self-hatreds outwards, or to assert themselves when they feel their authority has been questioned' (p. 1). Although Young-Bruehl's thesis is focused on political and social themes, her observations about the 'powerlessness' of children can be applied to the family contexts described here.

The thing with treating couples is that partners are seldom at the same level when dealing with serious developmental achievements, such as Oedipal and separation–individuation issues. If one partner is motivated, consciously and/or unconsciously, to individuate and the other is not, there will undoubtedly be more conflict in the relationship than if they are closely matched – unless one person's pulling the other away from the family of origin is part of the unconscious contract. In cases where they are not matched on this dimension, the striving partner may describe the relationship as suffocating, while the less-separated partner may describe it as insecure, and fear abandonment.

Because of this difference in 'readiness', in this case to separate from parents, it is common for one or both partners to be referred for simultaneous individual work. Nate was already in individual treatment; it was his therapist who referred the couple to me. In Nate's case, as the couples work progressed, he was able to terminate his individual therapy. In Caroline's case, as the work progressed, her individual therapy deepened. For Pamela and Tom, their separation issues from both their families were at close enough points and contributed to the relationship problems almost equally, although in different ways. Although they were seemingly matched on developmental achievements, or lack thereof, Pamela felt certain that she wanted to stay in the relationship, while Tom presented as being in the throes of anguished decision-making. Therefore, it seemed to all of us that Tom's issues needed to be worked through before any decision about the marriage could be made. Also, as he talked more about his lack of sexual attraction for Pamela, she was getting hurt, so a referral for individual treatment seemed very important. After the couples therapy, when Pamela better understood her own fears of adult intimacy, she also accepted a referral to individual treatment.

## Clinical vignette 3.3

One more interesting example: in another couple I saw, both from the same original city, shortly after their marriage the husband noticed that the wife was so involved with her original family that it interfered greatly with her attention to him. As he talked about it, we heard that she could do nothing right for this family and was expected to perform tasks and take on chores that no other sibling was asked to do. We came to refer to her as Cinderella. When one day the husband returned home to find his wife sitting on the floor of a closet, crying, he decided to step into this tortuous morass, and take action, and stated that they had to move out of town. One year later the couple moved to a different city, where they both restarted their careers. Two years after that, the wife's parents decided to move – to the same city – and bought a house two blocks away from where the couple lived. This brought them into treatment.

Because the Oedipal transference is usually diluted in couples therapy, the therapist is able, as a recognized external object, to offer both partners an alternative 'parent' and to highlight how these issues form obstacles to their intimate relationship. In the case of Pamela and Tom, for example, the partners needed to grow into sexual adulthood and to understand how their 'friendship' had helped them avoid the possibility of true adult intimacy. As their understanding deepened, they both became aware of wanting more in a relationship than they had in their current one. The technique of treating couples is elaborated in an earlier publication (Usher, 2008).

How much do separation issues in couples interfere with 'full frontal intimacy', as Stephen Mitchell (2002) put it? Or, maybe, how much are they put to use for that end?

## Affairs

As we can see, hurdles in developmental stages are often manifested in difficulties in forming a sustained, intimate relationship in adult life, and can present huge, and potentially miasmic, problems. Horney's statement cited earlier about men recoiling from the saintliness of women can sometimes be evidenced in the breaking away from the ongoing relationship by having an affair – for either partner. The 'Madonna–whore' representation can give relief from a mother- or father- or sibling-like choice in a partner, with libidinal energy hived off onto someone outside the relationship with whom it is easier to enjoy sex.

Affairs, I have learned, are like dreams and should be analysed by the people who created them. Their origins lie in the latent unconscious of the individuals involved (Usher, 2015). As in other matters of this sort, the therapist cannot know what is right or wrong, and what anyone should or should not do. Partly for this reason, when I treat couples, I always see both partners together. This avoids the game of 'I've got a secret', which, if permitted, paradoxically leaves the therapist in a position of decreased power, holding and withholding information.

The need to find someone outside the relationship can be linked to partners' difficulties with breaking away from their families of origin as often the spouse/long-term partner becomes synonymous with 'family'. Strain in the context of a pathologically unseparated husband is described in the next clinical vignette.

## Clinical vignette 3.4

Linda, a 42-year-old professional, and her husband Tony, also 42, came for treatment because Linda had an affair about one year earlier. She had finally told Tony about the affair, which she promised had ended, and he had become enraged and wanted to end their relationship. The affair had been brief and involved an unmarried work colleague, whom Linda had found irresistible. She had since left that job and had remained at home and out of the workforce.

This couple had met in high school in a small town, and married at age 19. They were both ambitious and wanted to improve their life circumstances. When they came for treatment, they had been married for over 20 years, living in a big city away from their families, and had no children, by mutual agreement. Both partners had difficult relationships with their families of origin.

Linda's father, an alcoholic, had been verbally abusive to her and her mother. When Linda was in her thirties, her mother, who had supported her husband faithfully, developed a brain tumour, and died after two years of illness. Linda had been having only sporadic contact with her widowed father when she came for treatment, as he had found a new partner.

Tony was from a very close Italian family. His father was also abusive, sometimes physically, and his mother was quite depressed. After his father died, five years before I met with them, his mother, who had never looked after herself, became a burden to Tony and to his sister, who still lived in the small town.

### Early treatment

In our beginning sessions, Tony's mother's expectations that he and Linda visit frequently, along with her very frequent phone calls, were described by Linda as 'gutting' their relationship. Tony had bought his mother a car and paid for repairs to her home, Linda informed me, and yet his mother called on those Sundays when they were not visiting and complained to him about how lonely and unhappy she was. She wore black all the time and visited his father's grave every day. Tony became angry and agitated after her phone calls. It took him many hours to settle down, thus, according to Linda, 'ruining our Sunday' – the only day they had sex, because of Tony's work schedule. 'His mother is now dictating our sex life', she said. 'I can't stand these phone calls. I will leave if he doesn't work this through.'

As we talked about their relationship, both indicated that they loved each other and wanted to stay together. Linda said, 'I would leave, but then if his mother died, I would want to go back to him', indicating her certainty that this was their only problem. As our work together progressed, it became evident to all of us that there were significant underlying issues for both of them, in addition to, or masked by, the problems with Tony's mother, especially pertaining to sexual intimacy. Still, one of Tony's main tasks during the therapy was to find a way to separate from his needy parent – which seemed impossible at first. The other was to forgive Linda for the affair.

Many of our beginning sessions focused on Tony's difficulties in separating from his mother. Although he was upset, even crying, throughout our beginning time together, he refused to seek individual therapy, wanting help from Linda to work this out. It took a long time for him to see that his ambivalent attachment to his mother reflected his attachment to Linda – needing her but hating her. Linda, for her part, was very angry and able to express herself easily in the sessions. She threatened to walk out of the treatment several times, just as she had threatened to leave Tony – which seemed realistic, considering that she now saw her affair as a reaction to Tony's mother problems. 'He had someone else, so I did too.' As Linda talked more about her strategy of leaving, she stated that it was the only way she knew to cope with difficult circumstances. When she had repeatedly witnessed her father verbally abusing her mother while she was growing up, she had left the house, feeling helpless – especially as her mother defended her father afterwards.

A major complaint was that Linda, who now did not work outside the home – partly at Tony's request – had a healthy appetite for sexual activity that Tony did not meet. He had a very demanding job at which he was highly successful; however, it seemed that he could not get his mother out of his psyche long enough to make love. By the time they came for treatment, in fact, Tony had been impotent sexually for more than six months. Our sessions were stormy, often involving a replication of the fights they had at home for me to witness. One of the difficulties in this treatment was to balance the airtime between the partners. Although it was obvious that Tony had problems resolving his guilt about not looking after his mother in the way to which she felt entitled, Linda's relationship to her family, now her father, was troubled in its own way. As she talked more about it, and about her telephone calls with her father, she described both of them as unable to communicate and crying in desperation. She had a strong and destabilizing reaction to her father's finding another woman. Linda needed a father and Tony needed a mother – but for both, not in the way they now had them, and not in the way they related to each other.

### Middle treatment

After the first few months of Linda's criticizing Tony – whom it became evident she had dragged into couples therapy to get 'fixed' – Linda was slowly able to express more of her disappointment in her father and, quite surprisingly, to allow Tony to help her. Of course, being married at such a young age, immediately after high school, each knew the other's family very well. Therefore, they were well equipped to understand the origins of the issues and knew, much better than I did, how their families had affected them. This is the marvel of work with couples – where three heads are often better than one, and where partners helping each other, as described in Clinical vignette 3.2 (Nate and Caroline), makes the work go more quickly; also, the effects are more lasting, since the other person is there and can remember and discuss the times in treatment, helping to put issues into perspective. In my role, I could be seen to be giving permission to Tony to set clear limits with his mother, while understanding how alone his mother must feel. As difficult as that part is, it is always more difficult, particularly in couples therapy, to help adult children examine their often archaic need for their parent.

## Clinical vignette 3.5

In another example, Janice and Bob, both in their early forties, had been having problems for some years when they came for therapy. Their sexual relationship had ended several years earlier, after the birth of their second child. Bob complained that he had always done the lion's share of the duties at home, in addition to his work outside the home. Janice also had a demanding job outside the home. This situation worsened when two years earlier, Janice's mother, who lived in another city, had become fatally ill, and Janice had spent whatever time she could at her mother's side until her death, about three months prior to their entering treatment. This illness, and Janice's preoccupation with it, had been the icing on an already bitter cake. Bob had felt relegated to the bottom of Janice's list of priorities (mother, children, job, Bob). Their complaints, in the beginning of treatment, were about doing household chores.

### Early treatment

About six months into treatment, they came to my office and rearranged my furniture. I have two chairs facing each other at an angle with a small round table in between. I sit opposite the chairs. Janice moved the table out of the way, put the two chairs very close together, and they held hands. She looked tired and very upset. 'Bob has had an affair.' Bob was crying, hiding his face in his hands.

I interpreted this rather unusual furniture rearranging behaviour as a defence against the fear of their marriage ending, and we began to explore the circumstances leading up to this situation. Janice had been very close to her mother (see the Quotable quotes at the end of this chapter). She had admired her and wanted to be like her. This idealizing stance – which we later understood as reactive to her guilt over her extremely rebellious adolescence and her fear that she had caused her mother's later illness – left Bob out in the cold of reality. He could not compete with a defence. Because of her extreme closeness to her mother, Janice had not only been emotionally distracted by the illness, but had been physically absent from the home for most weekends during those two years. Bob's affair had begun during the first year of Janice's absence.

The work of therapy involved our going back to the critical time of the cessation of their sexual relationship, after the birth of their second child. Janice had panicked at that time, feeling her life was slipping away, and had begun overindulging in exercise, dieting, and work, excluding Bob and the children. She desperately needed to get her own life back. She had confided in her mother, who agreed with her actions and said that she had felt the same way. This was the beginning of long telephone conversations and emails between them describing their various lots in life and encouraging each other. Janice's father had rarely been at home as he attended to his very demanding job, and her mother had felt very alone. Janice was relieved and happy to fill this void. She had no sexual desire that she was aware of, and spent her energy on her personal activities and, as much as was possible, on the children. This behaviour had caused Bob to feel angry and alienated.

Bob, for his part, came from a conventional, roast-beef-on-Sundays family, where everyone was cheerful. He had encountered serious difficulties at work during this time and worried that he might lose his job. Because of his family's requirement for cheerfulness, he had felt that he should not share his anxiety with Janice, who was otherwise preoccupied with her mother's fatal illness. The married woman with whom he had the affair understood his work problems, as she had worked at the same company, and also understood his marital dissatisfaction, as her marriage was also in trouble. They had spent many hours talking over coffee. Coffee had led to drinks. Drinks had led to bed.

Janice reported in our therapy that she had found romantic and highly detailed sexual emails from Bob to this other woman. She had confronted Bob and he had confessed to the affair, claiming it was over, even though it had still been ongoing after the couples therapy had begun. Nothing would suffice except for Janice to bring in the emails and read them aloud, rather dramatically, in our session. Humiliated, Bob was almost silent for the next few sessions.

Because of both partners' perception of the fragility of their relationship (see the beginning of this section), they were both resistant to describing the rage they had felt towards each other over the years. For Janice, the very recent loss of her mother had become conflated with her fear of losing her husband after learning about the affair, making the situation even more brittle. As they acknowledged that neither of them wanted to end the relationship, it gradually became easier for them to express the anger they had been feeling during the preceding years. Janice had felt treated like a child, in terms of running the household, and Bob had felt she behaved immaturely and selfishly by not doing her part, and was highly critical. Her absences for her mother's illness magnified what he saw as her lack of responsibility at home. He had been the good one; she had been the bad one. After the disclosure of the affair, Janice confessed that she was taking pleasure in having the upper hand at last, as Bob was the guilty party.

### Middle treatment

As the work went on, Janice was able to acknowledge how terrifying sustained intimacy had been for her, especially in the context of the 'scene' of a husband and two children. Bob came to see how the narcissistic injury of his work difficulties had been soothed by the excitement and overvaluation of the affair, and how his seeming lack of importance to Janice had justified this action. For both partners, the fall from grace of each in the eyes of the other – as the marriage continued and they were exposed to life together and the responsibilities inherent in having children – was hard to endure. They each found distractions (sick parent; affair).

For some partners in a romantic relationship, the shift from being swept away in the idealization of a new love to the reality of the actual person can be difficult, and sometimes impossible. Dicks (1967) describes this idealization as the main defence mechanism in couple relationships, as it makes love 'blind'.

Can we blame Janice's dying mother for Janice's strong attachment to her at the end that caused her to abandon her husband and children? That seems a bit much, even for this book. Yet, as we explored Janice's early family life, we heard how alone Janice thought her mother had felt at home, and how happy her mother had been to have experienced what seemed to be the resolution of Janice's rapprochement crisis after her defiant adolescence. As well, Janice's envy of her older brother, who had been the mother's favourite, was assuaged by this relatively new and intense connection with her mother. Her silent words to her mother were, 'I will always be there for you.'

## Summary

It is interesting to try to unravel the threads of attachment and separation in the patients described in Chapters 2 and 3. The educational and professional level that the patients here had achieved, which involved many years at school, could be said to have slowed their developmental growth; they had not been out in the adult world earlier, and possibly were financially dependent on parents.

In at least two of the cases described – that of Lily (Chapter 2) and Caroline – the mothers appeared, by description, to be quite disturbed, exhibiting borderline features, with difficulty in affect regulation. They were inconsistent, at best, in their capacity for concern. Caroline had memories of good times with her mother when she was very young, and had enjoyed the feeling of closeness with her, until she started to grow up; Lily could remember only one or two instances of happy times with her mother – she was so frightened of her mother's criticism that she could never relax with her. The fathers in these examples were either absent because of their silence and passivity (Lily), or had abandoned the family (Caroline). These experiences left both patients to find a mate who was not like mother, but also was not like father – a difficult task, which Caroline achieved better than Lily, perhaps having had that difference of early positive memories with her mother. In these situations, as has been referred to earlier, the mother appeared to be the damaging parent, although, if we were to ask ourselves what is missing from this picture, it would be both fathers, who had not done their 'job'.

What also seems to be common in these stories is that the parents have not considered the needs of their 'child' ahead of their own needs – even in some minimal way. In all of these cases, the offspring are regarded as just that – offspring. One hypothesis that emerged for me in considering these patients is that there is a generational component, not only in terms of the 'inheritance' factor, i.e. parents who have separation problems have difficulty allowing their children to separate. In the generation of these patients' parents (who were mostly in their seventies when the patients came for treatment), psychotherapy, and certainly psychoanalysis, was thought of as being for 'crazy' people; none of the parents had ever had the opportunity to work through the traumas that had unknowingly changed their lives. In most cases, they were not aware of how angry, unsatisfied, and sad they were, and certainly not aware of the effects of their mood on their family – as we supposedly are today. There are now significantly more people who are fortunate enough to have therapy before or during childrearing, to gain an understanding of their own problems and the possible effects of these issues on their new families.

There may be a swing in the next generation, however – in research and popular literature – in the direction of over-focusing on (and over-diagnosing) the needs of the child. This can trigger an over-concern in parents about the need to be better than good enough, as well as fuelling resentment and envy – and cause difficulties in letting go.

Another issue that has been referred to only in passing here is the effect of cultural and religious norms on separation–individuation. For these couples, and many others I have seen, their cultural backgrounds play a significant role in their psychic representation of separation. In couples of mixed race or religion, one partner may be 'ahead' or 'behind' the other in working through these issues and, indeed, as has been mentioned, may have connected with the other in order to help pull him or her out of the morass. Tony's connection to his Italian mother had a huge impact on his relationship with Linda. Pamela's relationship to her Chinese family, who were comfortable living in the home of their married daughter, also had a significant impact. Ben (Clinical vignette 2.3) had a strong commitment to his Orthodox Jewish family, which he used to impede his thinking of himself as a separate individual. There is, of course, the old joke: How is a Rottweiler different from a Jewish/Italian/Chinese (fill in the blank) mother? The Rottweiler eventually lets go of the kid.

Even same-race couples will encounter these difficulties because, of course, their family environments are different. In one couple I saw, both of whom were of second-generation East Indian extraction, the husband's parents denied their heritage by giving their son a Canadian name and encouraging him to integrate into Canadian (business) society as much as possible. The wife, on the other hand, whose name was identifiably Indian, was enmeshed with her family, particularly her (as it again happens) critical mother, and was expected to observe certain rules. This difference manifested itself in an extreme way when the husband's father expressed his disapproval of his son's marriage to this woman and refused to attend the couple's traditional Indian wedding.

## Quotable quotes

The following are quotable quotes from patients seen in couples therapy.

Janice, 41 (described in this chapter): *'When my mother died I lost my closest friend. She would tell me things she didn't tell my father, and I would tell her things I'd never tell Bob. Now there's no one.'*

Henry, 40, business analyst: *'My family is very close and that's the way it is – you have to accept it. Yes, we are in each other's laundry.'*

Maureen, 31, social worker: *'Doug's mother is still trying to win over Doug. I bought these boots, trying to look sexy for my husband. She asked me where I got them and then bought the exact same ones.'*

Tom, 40 (described in this chapter): *'Pamela has left her pension and life insurance to her brother. How can I possibly fit into this family, or get her to acknowledge me?'*

Jennifer, 35, lawyer: *'If John's mother and I were both drowning in a lake, I know he would save her first.'*

The above are true quotations – only the names have been changed to protect the unseparated.

## References

Cantor, D. W. (1982). Divorce: Separation or separation-individuation. *American Journal of Psychoanalysis, 42*, 307–313.

Dicks, H. V. (1967). *Marital tensions: Clinical studies towards a psychological theory of interaction.* London: Karnac.

Fairbairn, W. R. D. (1963). Synopsis of an object-relations theory of the personality. *International Journal of Psychoanalysis, 44*, 224–225.

Horney, K. (1967). *Feminine psychology.* New York: W. W. Norton.

Mitchell, S. A. (2002). *Can love last? The fate of romance over time.* New York: W. W. Norton.

Modell, A. H. (1965). On having the right to a life: An aspect of the superego's development. *International Journal of Psychoanalysis, 46*, 323–331.

Ruszczynski, S. (Ed.). (1993). *Psychotherapy with couples: Theory and practice at the Tavistock Institute of Marital Studies.* London: Karnac.

Usher, S. F. (2008). *What is this thing called love? A guide to psychoanalytic psychotherapy with couples.* London: Routledge.

Usher, S. F. (2015). Hope and hopelessness in the couple relationship. In S. Akhtar and M. K. O'Neil (Eds.), *Hopelessness: Developmental, cultural, and clinical realms* (pp.165–180). London: Karnac.

Young-Bruehl, E. (2012). *Childism: Confronting prejudice against children.* New Haven: Yale University Press.

# Chapter 4

# 'Home is where we start from'[1]

## The sibling connection

'But I don't *want* a baby sister!'

Thus begins the story of Little Hans, the five-year-old son of the musicologist Max Graf, whose sister's birth was seen to be 'the great event in Hans' life', and triggered, among other things, an interest in the differences between the sexes, in particular, widdlers (the penis). His father wrote to Freud, 'Hans is very jealous of the new arrival, and whenever anyone praises her, says she is a lovely baby and so on, he at once declares scornfully, "But she's not got any teeth yet"' (Freud, 1909, p. 11). By age five, Hans was able to tell his father that he thought, really wished, that his little sister might fall into the bathwater and die.

According to Bank and Kahn (1980–1981), who studied Freud's writings on siblings, Hans, as an older child, was not improved by having a younger child to whom he might be a teacher. Hannah simply threatened his monopoly over his parents' love. In this case, 'the sibling relationship has no separate life of its own' (p. 496). In terms of the Wolf Man, Bank and Kahn point out how the Wolf Man's older sister, Anna, made him feel inferior. Freud (1918) describes the Wolf Man's relationship to his sister as having triggered his phobia of wolves by frightening him with wolves in picture books, as well as seducing him sadistically, and rebuffing his sexual advances. In Freud's 'Totem and Taboo' (1913), Bank and Kahn point out that the brothers seem to have a bond only because they are working out their Oedipal guilt together, assassinating and eating their tyrannical father. These writers go on to discuss Freud's own experience as a brother, which, they state, was negative: he felt guilty about the death of his younger brother, Julius; he felt dominated by his step-brother's son, Philip; and he actively disliked his sister, Anna, who was closest to him in age.

The paucity of writing in this area is evidence that the developmental importance of siblings in the internal world of the individual has probably been, and continues to be, undervalued. We know that the traumas of sibling birth and sibling death have deep, usually life-long effects: siblings are, after all, unlike our parents, our lifelong companions. Yet in the psychoanalytic world there is still no clear paradigm through which we can understand these effects. Our theories are dominated by a vertical model, by patterns of descent and ascent: mother or father to child, and child to parent. 'Sibs are included [in the literature] among the members of the supporting cast in oedipal dramas, playing such roles as fantasized offspring, parent surrogates, additional rivals, or alternative objects' (Leichtman, 1985, p. 111).

However, analytic attention to sibling relationships is beginning to grow as analysts realize that analyses can stalemate if they do not pay attention to the unique influence of siblings, which is different from – and in some cases even more important than – that of parents. Rosner (1985) states that sibling relationships are of great significance to ego development, to structural defensive considerations, and to self and object representations; as well, he states that siblings are significant objects of internalization.

For the purposes of this book, I will examine the effect of siblings on the process of separation–individuation. Sibling rivalry, sibling affection, sibling aggression, the reparative function of siblings, sibling passion, identification with and differentiation from siblings, and the pathological features of sibling relationships all contribute not only to our choice of defences and the future of our object relationships, but also to the way we leave home – or not.

In an important article on siblings' attempts to separate from each other, Vivona (2007) writes, 'The lateral dimension of psychic life, lived through relationships with siblings and their substitutes, is structured around a distinct psychic challenge: to find one's unique place in a world of similar others. Like the challenge of structures in the vertical parent-child dimension, the lateral challenge is fraught with conflict and ambivalence' (p. 1191). Vivona states that the resolution of this conflict can be accomplished through what she calls a process of differentiation, where the child amplifies the differences with siblings and minimizes the similarities. She maintains that seeing sibling relationships as merely displaced from parental relationships short-circuits significant development processes.

Differentiation, like its counterpart identification, can ease sibling rivalry. However, differentiation has its down sides, too. Gillian, to be described in Clinical vignette 4.2, worked so hard at being different from a hyper-emotional younger sister that she unfortunately became distant and emotionally unavailable with peers and in romantic relationships.

## Sibling rivalry

Sibling rivalry, competition over a prize of love with rivals who are both loved and hated, signals the major challenge of the lateral dimension, as oedipal rivalry signals the major challenge of the vertical dimension.

(Vivona, 2007, p. 1194)

Parents, of course, have a crucial effect on sibling rivalry. When one child is praised and the other is not, victorious gloating in one leads to rage and resentment in the other. On the other hand, when parents, in a sometimes frantic attempt not to show favouritism, equate their children's talents and abilities, they may end up diminishing the talents of the more successful one so that no one is hurt, thereby potentiating the fantasy that a sibling/peer can be harmed by being defeated. This puts an obvious damper on competitive strivings, and individuating.

The literature on sibling rivalry has emphasized the negative effects of the often-unconscious murderous rage that first-born children have toward subsequent siblings, and is discussed within the context of the Oedipal situation, that is, love for and from the parents.

Taunting, unfavorable comparisons and preferences trigger guilt-ridden, hostile, vengeful, and jealous fantasies and feelings which have long-term effects upon ego development and upon the formation of object relations. Competitive strivings and fears of such strivings influence early instinctual development.

(Rosner, 1985, p. 457)

Rosner suggests that the effects of these experiences are greater when put into the context of Mahler's findings. If a sibling is born during the practising sub-phase, when the older child's narcissism is particularly fragile, the impact will not be the same as when the new baby comes following the rapprochement period, when the older child is more aware of his separateness.

In an important early article, Graham (1988) states that the psychoanalytic study of the developmental effects of siblings suffers from a 'contempt of familiarity', because these relationships are all around us – at home, in the clinic and in our societies. For many analysts there may be unconscious, unresolved feelings towards siblings, making this an uncomfortable area at which to look too closely. Graham writes, 'I contend that the sibling is both a developmental companion and a transference shaper' (p. 90). And, 'I found that the nature of these attachments often seems to be a better and more immediate indicator of the quality and potential of marital relationships than are the more distant and iconic relationships with the parents' (p. 92). If our own internalized sibling experience has not been analysed, we may not be equipped to analyse the sibling experience of our patients.

As Rustin (2007) describes, the sibling relationship can partially compensate for the lack of a positive holding environment. She sees siblings as having a sort of 'we ego'. The single child who is dealing with a new arrival and the rivalry inherent therein, at the same time gains a 'companion, and one who at times can be an ally in mischief and rebellious discontent with parental demands, as well as a playmate with whom a shared imaginary world can be created' (p. 27).

If there is no Oedipal strife, there is no growth. If there is no sibling strife/rivalry, there is almost no growth. In most cases for development to proceed, there must be conflict, which eventually becomes resolved.

Lily, the 41-year-old woman described in detail in Clinical vignette 2.2 (angry, emotional mother; depressed father), had an older brother, Rob. Because of his relatively outgoing, jokey character, Rob was usually the centre of attention in their home and in extended family gatherings. In their early years, Rob tormented, teased and even repeatedly punched Lily, while their mother made noticeably weak attempts to stop him, often laughing. Agger (1988) notes that borderline parents are especially prone to using the primitive defences of splitting and projective identification to induce conflict behaviours among their children in order to generate destructive patterns of relatedness to gratify their own aggressive needs.

When Lily's brother's teasing began, in concert with her mother's unconscious collusion, Lily would retreat to her room – when she could – and, feeling so intruded upon by both her mother and her brother, would fantasize having the courage to ask for a lock for her next birthday. This all occurred before the age of puberty for both Lily and Rob. As time went on, however, the siblings' reaction to their mother, who filled the family space with her unmodulated affect, seemed to trump the libidinous pleasure of the rivalry for Rob, and the masochistic pleasure of the pain of humiliation for Lily. By the time they were young teenagers, this rivalry was sublimated into an affectionate friendship, partly because Rob's sexuality and aggression could be directed outside the home, and partly because they needed each other in the face of their mother's aggression.

In the familiar German folk story of Hansel and Gretel, a young brother and sister are threatened by a cannibalistic witch living deep in the forest, and save their lives by outwitting (killing) her. The teasing, as bad as it was, seemed for Lily to be the lesser of two 'evils', as she described that she and Rob were like these children, supporting each other through the troubled family times. They even had their own code language, which they spoke so fluently and quickly that their parents could not understand them. They solved their sibling rivalry at this point in their development by identifying with each other – for example, they enjoyed the fact that people who called their home could not tell their voices apart.

As Lily and Rob became young adults, Rob was unable to tolerate their father's waning energy and his thickening depression. Since he had a link with their mother (his own aggression), it was more natural for him to deny some of her hostility, especially when he was only occasionally the target. Rob was not as enmeshed with either parent as Lily – not as frightened by their mother and not consciously worried about their father – and therefore he found it easier to separate from the family. He managed to extricate himself from much of the family drama by going out and encouraged Lily to do the same, but she could not.

There was another disturbing 'sibling' obstacle to leaving home that affected Lily, contributing to her insecure attachment to her mother, and that confirmed for Lily that she could never have her mother's love. Lily's mother, as was mentioned in Chapter 2, was pathologically envious of her own younger sister who actually had the same name as her daughter (Lily) – another wrinkle. This sister also had two children, an older boy and a younger girl. In a primitive attempt to overcome her destructive envy of her sister, Lily's mother, thanks to an overactive use of reaction formation, was conscious only of an extreme idealization of her sister and of her sister's children. She brought a phantom sibling into the home: another daughter, the daughter of her sister, but one who was 'perfect' in every way. Lily was expected to wear her cousin's handed-down clothes, even when they did not fit, and to make the same choices in her life as her cousin. Lily's inability to have children, as her cousin had done, confirmed for Lily that she was deeply deficient and therefore unlovable and probably 'rotten to the core', as her mother had told her. This repeated comparison contributed greatly to Lily's very low self-esteem and to feelings of lack of entitlement, which bound her even more closely to her mother – trying, against all odds, to be seen as at least equal to her cousin. In a different personality constellation – perhaps with active paternal support – people like Lily would have felt entitled to a better life and would have left home as soon as they could. Using Vivona's (2007) concept of differentiation from her phantom sib in a positive way, instead of feeling less than her, Lily would have acknowledged the (obvious) differences in their academic achievements and in their capacity to care for others. Lily's brother, Rob, did try to help with this bizarre situation, by pointing out to their mother regularly, but in a logical manner, how Lily was superior to their cousin. Even though his protests were helpful validation for Lily, his opinion on this matter did nothing to loosen their mother's defences.

In our work to understand Lily's inability to become pregnant as an adult, we could now add Lily's attempt to differentiate herself from her mother and this cousin (femininity; reproductive capacity) as another psychological contributor. The guilty rage and jealousy aroused by her mother's splitting between her (bad) and her cousin (good) may also have led to self-defeating, masochistic behaviour in this sensitive arena as well as to a feeling of stubborn rebellion, complicated by her conscious sense of being less than those women who had managed to reproduce. Another 'sibling' contributor may have been Lily's inability to consolidate her femininity by establishing a firm identity separate from her idealized brother – whom she felt she needed in what seemed like a soul-threatening family environment (see Gabbard, 2009). (Of course, an inability to conceive may be due to many physiological factors; however, it was interesting to contemplate with Lily what the possible psychological influences might have been.)

Positive sibling influence can often be augmented in families where one or both parents are angry, depressed or absent through death, divorce or physical illness. In the case described above, both parents were compromised in their ability to parent: Lily's mother, because of her lack of ability to modulate her affect; Lily's father, because of his depression. Later in their development, siblings can act as active models for each other, influencing the post-adolescent development of ideals and values, as well as offering solutions for traditional family problems.

Rosner (1985) writes that instances in which a sibling has served as an antidote to pathological parenting are well-known. Another patient I saw had a father diagnosed with manic-depressive illness when he was in Oedipal time. His mother's unhelpful tag line when his father was in a manic state was 'Pay no attention', which underlined everyone's hopelessness about the situation. This patient suffered from excruciating shyness and embarrassment due to his father's behaviour, and to his unconscious fantasies of an Oedipal victory – saving his mother from this terrifying man. For these fantasies to come to fruition, however, he would have had to get rid of an older brother, who not only got there first, but who seemed more able to be competent at taking care of the family. This brother was described as 'calm and mature' by comparison to their out-of-control father, and was highly regarded in the community of their small town, where the family situation was evident. Although this patient was consciously relieved that his brother had taken over, his frustrated Oedipal desires became manifest in later life in intense free-floating anxiety, bouts of depression and an inability to find a work self.

## Teasing and bullying

Diana, the 50-year-old mild-mannered artist who was described in Clinical vignette 2.4, was the youngest by several years of three siblings. Her sister, who was seven years older than her, was a rebellious child as a teenager, often causing loud fights at home and staying out overnight from the time she was 15 years of age. When her distressed parents expressed anger and hopelessness about her sister's behaviour, Diana actually took notes with a pen and paper, outlining for herself what not to do. This was the beginning of her attempts at differentiation. To add to her problems with establishing a differentiated self, Diana's brother, four years her senior, who was often berated by their father for not measuring up to his expectations, used his little sister as an object for the displacement of his reaction to his father's critical assaults. In this situation, the older brother's teasing had a similar effect as in the case of Lily, described above; here, however, the patient's father joined in the teasing, and her mother was, for all intents and purposes, silent. The self-esteem of both these younger children was significantly damaged.

Diana remembered that from the time she was about six years of age until puberty, her brother would hold her down and tickle her aggressively until she felt sick; he also tickled her under her arm every time she reached up, so that she developed the habit of protecting her underarm with her other hand when reaching for something, which she continued into adulthood. The teasing and bullying contributed to Diana's hiding her considerable artistic talent and damping down her desires. She told me, 'My urges and talents are in a basement box with a key.' She discovered very early that it was not worth expressing her own passions as she would be humiliated, and so she kept everything to herself. Later in life, she made tentative strivings toward her career – tentative because of her lack of confidence in being a separate, competent, adult woman. To unconsciously assure that she would not rise too far, she married a man who interfered with her growth in a different way, by showing himself to be incapable of looking after their children if she were to pursue her chosen field. In the case of both Lily and Diana, the shame of having been the object of abuse and humiliation had a powerful and paralyzing effect on their ability to move forward. Both Lily and Diana allowed their older siblings to feel victorious over them, time after time. As their treatment progressed, they became more aware of their own talents, and particularly of how they had minimized, and indeed buried, their talents to maintain their relationship with their older siblings and to avoid the pain they felt would result if they did not. The excavation of their long-buried wishes to see the light of day, although tentative at first, was terribly exciting. Some strife is necessary; too much makes for curtailment of growth.

## Sibling desire

Perhaps it is time to re-evaluate whether it is the parents who are always the prototype for romantic relationships, as in, 'Did she marry her father or her mother?'. We often see patients who have modelled themselves, their friendships and their romantic relationships on their siblings. Freud describes the Wolf Man as turning to a servant girl, who had the same name as his sister, to meet the needs of his maturing sexuality after being rejected by Anna. 'In doing so, he was taking a step which had a determinant influence upon his heterosexual object choice. For all the girls with whom he subsequently fell in love – often with the clearest indications of compulsion – were also servants whose education and intelligence were necessarily far inferior to his own' (Freud, 1918, p. 23), although, for Freud, these sibling effects were always understood as *derivative* of the Oedipal struggle. Abend (1984) confirms that the prevailing view of sibling fantasies has been that they are only secondary formations – a less threatening derivative of incestuous wishes that involve the parents. On the other hand, Agger (1988) writes,

> The formulation of the Oedipus complex, in addition to its scientific merit, may have served a neurotic need for a cognitive vehicle to which one could attach a disturbing constellation of primitive feelings. To discover incestuous wishes and murderous fantasies towards parents may have been *less* distressing than to experience them in connection with siblings, where the sadistic component and castration anxiety may be more intense.
>
> (Agger, 1988, p. 12; emphasis mine)

I would add – and are at greater risk of actually being acted out. Abend (1984) agrees that powerful sibling love can leave an ineradicable stamp on the pattern of object choice later in life. Abend's patient had an older sister who was immature and seductive and devoted to him. It was only after she left home that he was able to masturbate. When he finally dated, he acted with women as he had with his sister, behaving like the kid brother.

In a recent comprehensive review of the literature on siblings, Haas-Lyon (2007) states that, out of the writing of earlier authors, we have an understanding that siblings are significant internal objects, that the feelings associated with them can be 'excruciatingly intense and ambivalent ... The intense guilt about murderous and incestuous wishes toward siblings may result in guardedness or profound inhibitions in strivings' (p. 6). She goes on to remind us that pathological sibling relationships often affect Oedipal resolution and separation and individuation. Sadistic acting out (e.g. teasing) can often serve as a defence against forbidden sexual desire, whether in siblings of the same or opposite sex, as can idealization.

## Clinical vignette 4.1

Sam was a 38-year-old married man who had emigrated from Europe to Toronto five years before coming to therapy, with his wife and two children. He was referred to me by his wife's therapist. His complaint was that his wife was 'crazy' and that no one in his family liked her. His mother, in particular, thought his wife was taking advantage of him, and his sister, who was divorced, thought his wife was an angry person and that he could have 'done better'. Even though he no longer lived in his home country with these family members, their accusations affected him deeply.

About one year before coming to see me, he had started an affair with a single colleague at work, who had a higher level position than his, and whom he described as a 'goddess'. He introduced her to me by way of a photograph on his iPhone for confirmation. I noticed that this woman dressed in a highly provocative manner at work, where they carried on an erotic email and text correspondence.

As our therapy went on, the topic of Sam's divorced sister came up. Sam acknowledged that he and his sister were very close. He said, 'She is beautiful; she is a goddess.' When I reminded him of the description he had given me of the woman at work, he said, 'Yes. They're both goddesses.' He then showed me a picture of his sister, who, in my opinion, was attractive, but not a 'goddess'. In fact, I commented to him that she looked more like him than like his lover. Sam said, 'Yes. We're twins!'.

Trying to suppress the interpretations that were pulsing through my analytic cortex (a much under-researched part of the brain), I began by describing, in plain terms, the concept of narcissistic object choice. It was a long haul; eventually, the therapy, along with his wife's threat to leave him – probably in equal proportions – led to his giving up his lover and beginning to work on his marriage.

## Clinical vignette 4.2

Another young woman I was seeing was planning to marry into a very tight European family, and had always felt on the outside in reaction to her husband's relationship to his sister. In this family, the parents' divorce had left the mother so embittered that she would not allow her children to see their father. As a result of this disruption, my patient's husband and his sister had become very close. The sister married first and had children; before the brother's marriage, he spent many evenings at her home – after his marriage, less so. This man consulted his sister first about important matters, and explained to my patient that his sister relied on him. After my patient married him, she found a shirt he had kept, given to him by his sister. The shirt had many handwritten quotations on it, of the type that encourage one to be brave and happy in life. At the bottom of the back of the shirt was a big 'lipstick kiss'.

Philip Haas's beautiful film, *Angels and Insects*, based on A. S. Byatt's novella *Morpho Eugenia* – the name of an exotic species of butterfly – takes us into the life of an aristocratic family in Victorian England in the 1860s, at a point when a naturalist scientist, who shares the same interest in insects as the father of the family, arrives on their doorstep, penniless, having lost all his Amazon specimens in a shipwreck – except for a few of his rare butterflies. William (Mark Rylance), our hero, is the perfect family outsider: polite and gracious, and always the Darwinian student. The story is deceptively simple: William falls in love with the melancholy oldest daughter, fortuitously named Eugenia (Kristin Scott Thomas). As the layers of complexity are added, William is told that Eugenia is sad because the man she was engaged to had died. William courts her with butterflies and wins her love, and even though, or perhaps because, he is told that her fiancé did not want to marry her, he is emboldened to ask for her hand. William then joins this household – and its massive grounds, which no one leaves throughout the duration of the film – but he is obviously still an outsider. He continues to study ants and other insects, taking the children on nature walks on the property. We soon begin to feel that something is deeply wrong in this household. The antagonist, Eugenia's brother and supposed protector, Edgar (Jeremy Kemp), despises William from the start and constantly reminds him that he is not part of this wealthy family. After her marriage to William, Eugenia produces a series of blonde babies (William has dark hair), and the audience, at least, starts to get suspicious. Then, in a stunning scene towards the end of the film, William is called back from a fox hunt and finds his wife, Eugenia, having passionate intercourse with her brother, Edgar, in the marital bed. Eugenia explains, 'This has been ever since I was little. It was something secret – like other things you're not supposed to do, and do.' We see how the metaphors of the ant and other insect colonies mirror the household. Insects have become incest. William leaves.

There are many paradoxes in this movie – the beauty of the film, the fascination of the insects, the lush house and gardens, and the original music, all lulling us into lovely mindlessness, only infrequently interrupted by the drunken ravings of the bad guy (Edgar). But as we continue watching, this beauty is revealed to exist in stark contrast to the horror: the shattered taboo, the ongoing relationship of which all the servants in the house are aware – in fact, of which everyone it seems is aware, undoubtedly including Eugenia's hysterical mother and possibly her obsessional father – except William.

Although this film portrays a particularly dramatic situation, there is often evidence in clinical practice of powerful sibling love, whether or not it is consummated, as is common in history, legend and literature. Freud (1913), in describing the lives of naked cannibals, states,

> Yet we find that they set before themselves with the most scrupulous care and the most painful severity the aim of avoiding incestuous sexual relations. Indeed, their whole social organization seems to serve that purpose or to have been brought into relation with its attainment.
>
> (Freud, 1913, p. 2)

In *Siblings: Sex and Violence* (2003), Juliet Mitchell reminds us that sexual and murderous wishes are present in all sibling relationships. Like Eugenia in Haas's film, Mitchell states, 'Most obviously, we have all taken on board that we must not commit incest – the hysteric in all of us wants to do just that, wants to do whatever is not allowed' (p. 5). Mitchell makes the distinction that incest with siblings is not for procreative purposes, but for sexual stimulation – that no one wants a baby. Perhaps this is why, in Haas's film, we are even more horrified when a succession of blonde babies appear.

When we think about how much time siblings normally spend together – and are reminded that they will potentially continue to have contact for almost their entire lives – we can begin to appreciate that there may actually be a separate line of development operating instead of, or along with, the relationship to the parents.

Several authors have noted that, along with the often ambivalent and conflicted relations of siblings, the role of the sibling as mirror and model has been less fully explored. As in the example of Lily, we can see the role of sibling solidarity in ameliorating the effect of inadequate or destructive parenting. Agger (1988) notes that a good-enough sibling may serve as a valuable 'looking-glass self' who allows the child to modify and contain himself in a sheltered environment, and states that it is helpful to have these scaled-down models after which to pattern oneself. Kieffer (2008) points out that the sibling bond has unique features of its own, distinguishing it from the hierarchical structure of the parent–child relationship. She notes that the 'more beneficent aspects of sibling relationships, includes their function in the regulation of psychological states and their potentiation of mutual recognition through encounters with one's first peers' (p. 161).

## Separation from siblings

Separation–individuation from siblings is distinct from what occurs with parents and has its own, often convoluted, line of development.

> These multivaried combinations of sibling enmeshments seem to require their own specific form of resolution ... in analysis, which leads to release from the attachment and an augmented sense of individuation from the sibling, together with the formation of new relationships to peers, colleagues, partners.
>
> (Kieffer, 2008, p. 100)

Sue, the handicapped woman described in Clinical vignette 1.1, had an older brother who, being safely ahead of her in almost every way growing up, was able to take the role of caring mentor, in part a defence against his jealousy of Sue's quite legitimate claim to extra attention from their parents. As it turned out, during our work together, Sue's separation from her parents was effected more easily than the separation from her brother; that is, her parents, who had looked after her and worried about her through her early years, were more able to recognize her as a competent adult than was her brother – possibly because of their lack of conscious guilt and somewhat lessened unconscious hostility. As was described in Chapter 1, over the time Sue was in treatment, they gradually adjusted their role with her, quite happily visiting her for their own purposes and not to take care of her.

With her brother, things seemed more complicated. Sue said that her older brother had always cared for her in a supportive way that she appreciated, and she trusted him implicitly (brother = good; parents = bad). As she began to move forward, however, she was not only surprised to notice how her parents tried to move with her, but also how her brother began making derogatory comments to her. As Sue matured, it became evident that she was brighter intellectually, and more academically inclined, than her older brother. Sue had great difficulty allowing herself to be the one to progress in university and then in graduate school, but managed to do it, keeping a twinship transference alive with her brother. 'We like the same things; we react in the same ways.' She needed to keep him as her protector and to avoid injuring him narcissistically. He maintained that he was 'proud' of her and, indeed, he did help her as an adult by fixing things in her apartment, and giving her rides at times when she needed them. Since he seemed to be experiencing survivor guilt in reaction to having a handicapped sibling and to his unconscious desire to get rid of her when they were growing up, this brother needed to retain the comfortable mentor facade and to continue to perceive Sue as needing help. Therefore, he refused to recognize the changes that were occurring. His response confused Sue, who had imagined that he would always be supportive, even in her progress.

Things began to change when her brother married. At first, the couple included Sue on vacations, as this was her brother's conscious wish. They often took cruises, where Sue and her brother would leave the boat to explore, and her brother's wife would prefer the spa on board. These adventures were used to re-emphasize how alike they were – different from his wife. Treading on mined territory, they seemed oblivious to the explosion about to happen. Sue's brother's wife soon became angry about being left out of this twosome and tired of hearing how Sue needed help. She was cold to Sue and could be arbitrarily hostile to her, at first inadvertently playing a role in prying the siblings apart. As we began to understand Sue's sister-in-law's behaviour toward her, it became clearer that not only was she feeling left out, but also that she was serving as the vehicle for expressing her husband's unconscious hostility towards his sister, which he could never allow himself to acknowledge because of her disability. Gaining this understanding allowed Sue to shift in the way she related to her brother, to realize that she, too, needed to be separate from him, in order to be able to grow as much as she could – even if it was 'past' him – and she initiated a non-aggressive process of separation that was helpful to them both. In this case, the younger, 'disabled' sibling was, eventually and with help, able to pass her older brother, academically, financially and psychologically.

Separating from a sibling is an interesting factor in the separation–individuation process. In the above example, the sibling, although sometimes helpful in separation issues, himself needed to be separated from. In Lily's case, her relationship with her older brother provided reality testing and help with leaving; however, she then felt she must be so grateful to him, and so 'admiring' of him, that it was difficult to leave him psychologically, and therefore to potentially 'pass' him in her achievements. In Diana's case, as in Sue's case, although the older brothers had a negative effect on their self-esteem and confidence, both managed to separate from their brothers and to make a place for themselves in the world. In both those cases, the younger siblings attended university while their older siblings did not. Sue persevered with her studies and gained career competence; Diana married and had two intelligent and talented children, while her older brother was not able to sustain a long-term relationship. Interestingly, all three of these sisters – Lily, Sue and Diana – expressed a conscious overconcern about their older brothers' well-being, partly defending against their hostility for the way they were treated as children, and partly compensating for the guilt they felt for doing better in life.

## Clinical vignette 4.3

Gillian, a 38-year-old highly successful professional, of European background, came for therapy because her mother felt she was depressed. Both parents were professionally educated, and divorced when Gillian was nine years of age. The parents shared visits every two weeks with Gillian and her sister, who was three years older than her. Gillian described herself as being close to her mother, but having great difficulty tolerating her sister, whom she described as 'expressive and loud. I'm the opposite – I can't stand those displays'. When we began treatment, Gillian's sister had moved back home with their mother after minor surgery, and, in fact, left only near the end of our three years together. Their mother, who was enmeshed with her own demanding mother whom she was charged to care for, was no help in Gillian's relationship with her sister, as she herself was often 'frightened' by her older daughter's outbursts of rage. Gillian, who was used to containing her own feelings was, at first, quite reticent to talk about her family in therapy, and I thought she would find the work difficult. However, as we progressed, Gillian welcomed the time and asked for longer sessions, often demonstrating mild pressure of speech as evidence that she had so much to talk about.

By our third month, the main topic in therapy was Gillian's older sister. She did not use her name, but stated, 'She says awful things – cries and screams – then becomes the victim and weeps.' She was soon able to acknowledge that her sister's behaviour was a 'family secret' and that everyone was held hostage by it. Growing up, Gillian's sister had been quite manipulative with her, declaring how much she loved Gillian, and that she wanted them to be 'close'. This behaviour caused Gillian significant pain, as she felt she should feel the same, and she longed for a close relationship with her sister; however, she was repulsed by her sister's unpredictable histrionics.

It wasn't long into our work before I started calling hatred, 'hatred', and murderous wishes, 'murderous wishes'. Gillian herself could not use those words until later; however, once she did, stories of how she felt invisible at home tumbled out. She stated she could not see any solution to the hold her sister had on the family except for 'something to happen to her'.

Within the first six months of treatment, Gillian was able to leave her mother's home, and started to feel that perhaps her problems with her sister were becoming resolved. This all seemed straightforward; however, when Gillian's sister began to think about leaving the city, Gillian found herself alarmingly bereft. She explained that she was at fault for the status of their relationship because she was 'cold and unemotional'. We were then presented with the opportunity to begin to work through Gillian's need for her sister, along with the shame and guilt she felt for her reaction to her.

The relationship with her sister affected Gillian's difficulty with friendships, which mirrored, in part, the sister she could not trust. As we know, in a complex way, peers replace siblings. Her sister's behaviour was also explained as the reason Gillian was reluctant to invite anyone home, as in addition to the unpredictable histrionics, her sister had a tendency to take over her friends. Her sister's actions also muddied the waters in her relationship with her mother, who later recruited Gillian into a spousal position, calling her frequently, complaining about her sister's abuse and manipulations and asking for problem-solving advice. And, of course, it affected her relationships with men – which, until this time, had been mostly platonic. As we explored this more deeply, it became clearer that Gillian's intense ambivalence about her sister had led to a sexual interest in women – who were seen as more exciting, and certainly more unpredictable, than men. This was reflected in the transference, as Gillian began dressing up for her sessions, sometimes swinging one leg over her chair as she talked, and asking personal questions. Of course, it was reflected in the counter-transference as well. Rereading my notes, I see that I wrote, 'Gillian looked great today'. Because of her intelligence and her contained manner, I found her attractive and looked forward to our time together.

Through our work, Gillian was able to acknowledge her envy of her sister's ability to express emotions, and also of her success in getting their mother's attention. She ventured out to establish a relationship with her estranged father, with whom she found she had much in common. Her father – belatedly – helped Gillian to remove herself from the entanglement of her mother and sister. She began to enjoy her work more and to consider adopting a baby, as she wanted a child and felt hopeless about finding a male partner. This plan helped her to see herself as starting a separate family.

In this situation, the sibling relationship interfered with the process of separation–individuation, complicated by the patient's relationship with both her parents. Gillian's mother put her in the competent, problem-solving role, where her mother needed her to be, ignoring Gillian's need for support and caretaking, and put her other child in the role of needy baby to be taken care of – which she also needed. Their father, who undoubtedly could have changed this dynamic, had escaped early and had very little influence on his daughters' developing emotional lives.

It is evident that separating from a sibling, particularly when the sibling is the object of intense feelings, is another important facet of separation–individuation. Siblings serve so many functions: they are our first 'others', they provide company and companionship growing up, they are a mirror, they validate or invalidate our perceptions, they are our reflections of reality – telling us, sometimes all too honestly, how we look, how we behave. When we do not have a sibling, or even when we do, we may have an imagined sibling or siblings – sometimes a fantasy twin – conscious or unconscious, to assuage the lack of mirroring and the loneliness of childhood. Siblings are our lifelong companions. As such we need to recognize that our patients' siblings are not just the supporting cast in the Oedipal drama, but often have starring roles.

## Birth order

Birth order, including gender, although not the focus of this chapter, obviously plays a role in sibling relationships and their movement toward separation. The experience of the older sibling is often as a buffer, or intermediary, between the parents and the younger sibling(s), and they may also serve as a buffer between the parents. Depending on the state of the parents' marriage when the older sibling/first child is born, they may be seen by the parents as a welcome addition, or as an intruder (see Pamela and Tom, Clinical vignette 3.1). Either way, their presence changes the dynamics of the couple, and they may sense this unconsciously. The older child is the original third in the couple, taking away their time and privacy. This can lead to a sense of responsibility, not only for their younger siblings, but for their parents as well (S. Sadavoy, private communication). It may happen – especially in marriages that are not mutually satisfying – that the mother invests all her libidinal energy in her first baby. This excludes the husband, and the child may be pulled unwittingly into the marital problems. One patient I saw recently, whose husband had a demanding job that took him away from home frequently, was accused by him of falling in love with their little son, and caring more for the baby than for him. He unfortunately became verbally abusive to the child and intolerant of typical childish behaviours. This led to tension between the parents, which lasted many years. Despite other children arriving on the scene, this man was unable to connect with his first son, causing the son to initially cling to his mother for protection, and then as the other children were born, to strike out on his own, as much as he could. It appears that this child will achieve separation in a way that is different from his younger siblings, either by making excessive use of the secure base provided by his mother and trying to ingratiate his father, so lingering longer, or by exercising a premature stab at independence.

The older ('murderous') child or children can sometimes have a more significant effect on the separation of younger siblings from the mother than does the father. Despite (or because of) the taunting and teasing, older siblings of both sexes often have considerable influence in helping younger ones to separate. Leichtman (1985) states, 'Older siblings play a major role in early identity formation and object relationships, a role that, while affected by relationships with parents, is also important, independent of those relationships' (p. 156). In fact, one of the most important forces acting upon an individual's success or lack thereof in separating from parents can be having an older sibling who paves the way – sometimes with a tank – and either by role modelling or with active encouragement helps the younger sibling(s) to do the same. Older siblings are usually under greater pressure from the parents to perform – academically and/or athletically – which may lead to better and quicker success in the outside world. On the other hand, older siblings may teach their younger siblings cognitive and psychomotor skills so that younger siblings may emerge ahead of their peers.

We have probably all seen older siblings in our practice who feel they must continually scramble to keep ahead of younger ones to such a degree that they can never reach the stage of friendly companionship with them. These individuals often carry this behaviour into relationships with peers, which may make them unpleasant to be with (the 'know-it-alls'). There is a syndrome I have called unconscious plagiarizing syndrome (UPS), in which older siblings take the statements, opinions and knowledge of the younger sibling and claim it as their own, declaring what might have been expressed quietly, in a more assertive manner, with no attribution. It happens so quickly that no one is aware of it – no one, that is, except the younger sibling. This can be seen in work situations and romantic relationships as well, depending on the transference reactions that are evoked. If an older sibling cannot tolerate the gains or good ideas of a younger sibling, they may be dismissive, as a defence against their envy, or become aggressive. When this is in the context of a family, of course it must be understood in terms of what is happening in the family at that time – mainly vis-à-vis the parents; if this happens at work, the environment and culture of the workplace offer clues to the person's motivation. An older sibling may never be able to acknowledge the successes and competencies of younger siblings, even when they are in an area in which they themselves have no interest.

The feeling of the younger ('victim') sibling is often that they must adopt a continually learning, non-threatening position – which some younger siblings do so horribly well – so as not to threaten the narcissism of the older sibling and perhaps lose the relationship. Idealizations by younger siblings of older siblings serve several purposes: the younger ones imagine they are looked after and protected (in Lily's case, from her mother; in Sue's case, from the world at large); they know their place as being second, or less than, and therefore can excuse themselves from the rigours of growing up, keeping the family in peaceful status quo; and they are able to indulge dependency and twinship needs, hearing barely a murmur of their own need to break out.

Sometimes a younger sibling may see themselves as hopelessly 'behind', feeling they will never do as well as others outside the family – even when it is explained to them that they were behind earlier because of being younger: that they did not have the same physical coordination or cognitive skills as their older sibling *at that time*. Younger siblings may also hold onto the memory of 'normal' teasing, perhaps because it was a way of garnering parental attention in the past, and therefore spitefully refuse to see their sibling as a companion in later life. A younger sibling may have some role in facilitating separation for the older one by 'holding the fort' while the older one escapes, or, possibly, unconsciously adding to the annoyance and restrictions of family life and thereby helping to catapult the older sibling out.

Sibling transferences are often expressed as rivalry with the analyst – sometimes professionally, sometimes in taste in clothing or even with reference to office décor. One of my patients who had a stormy relationship with a younger sibling commented on my yellow office as making everyone look yellow – a very unflattering colour, she assured me. Or, an attitude of proposed friendship or twinship that functions to deny the position of the analyst may be in evidence. An erotic or seductive response to the analyst's person emanating from unconscious incestuous sibling desires, or a masochistic victim-like submission to the analyst's interpretations emanating from sibling teasing can serve doubly as important information and as a resistance to the treatment. Knowing the role siblings have played in our patients' lives alerts us to these possible transference manifestations.

Pleading for a new metapsychology that would conceptualize sibling relations as relatively independent, autonomous structures, Mitchell states, 'Everyone always, of course, knew about the importance of siblings but linking them to everybody's actual or potential pathology, to the depths of our loves and lives, hates and deaths, opens up a rich vein of enquiry' (p. ix). Analytic attention to sibling relationships is now growing as we realize that analyses can stalemate if we do not pay attention to the unique influence of siblings – different, and in some cases, even more powerful – than that of parents.

## Quotable quotes

Vietnamese proverb: *'Brothers and sisters are as close as hands and feet.'*
Marc Brown (children's author): *'Sometimes being a brother is even better than being a superhero.'*
Author unknown: *'A friend is a brother who once was a bother.'*

Amy Li, artist/photographer: *'Having a sister is like having a best friend you can't get rid of.'*

Charles M. Schulz: *'Big sisters are the crab grass in the lawn of life.'*

Marian Salamaier, professor: *'A sibling may be the keeper of one's identity, the only person with the keys to one's unfettered, more fundamental self.'*

## Note

1 This title is taken from Winnicott's book (1986) of the same name.

## References

Abend, S. M. (1984). Sibling love and object choice. *Psychoanalytic Quarterly, 5*, 425–430.

Agger, E. M. (1988). Psychoanalytic perspectives on sibling relationships. *Psychoanalytic Quarterly, 8*, 3–30.

Bank, S. and M. D. Kahn (1980–1981). Freudian siblings. *Psychoanalytic Review, 67*, 493–504.

Freud, S. (1909). *Analysis of a phobia in a five-year-old boy,* S. E. 10.

Freud, S. (1913). *Totem and taboo,* S. E. 13.

Freud, S. (1918). *From the history of an infantile neurosis,* S. E. 17.

Gabbard, G. O. (2009). What is a 'good enough' termination? *Journal of the American Psychoanalytic Association, 57*(3), 575–594.

Graham, I. (1988). The sibling object and its transferences: Alternate organizer of the middle field. *Psychoanalytic Inquiry, 8*, 88–107.

Haas-Lyon, S. (2007). To outdo or undo? Siblings and hysteria. *Studies in Gender and Sexuality, 8*, 1–26.

Kieffer, C. C. (2008). On siblings: Mutual regulation and mutual recognition. *Annals of Psychoanalysis, 36*, 161–173.

Leichtman, M. (1985). The influence of an older sibling on the separation–individuation process. *Psychoanalytic Study of the Child, 40*, 111–161.

Mitchell, J. (2003). *Siblings: Sex and violence.* London: Blackwell.

Rosner, S. (1985). On the place of siblings in psychoanalysis. *Psychoanalytic Review, 72*, 457–477.

Rustin, M. (2007). Taking account of siblings: A view from child psychotherapy 1. *Journal of Child Psychotherapy, 33*, 21–35.

Vivona, J. M. (2007). Sibling differentiation, identity development, and the lateral dimension of psychic life. *Journal of the American Psychoanalytic Association, 55*(4), 1191–1215.

Winnicott, D. W. (1986). *Home is where we start from: Essays by a psychoanalyst.* New York: W. W. Norton.

# Chapter 5

# Out of the woods

## Treatment pauses and termination

### Breaks

Breaks in treatment for holidays, illness or professional commitments are always indicators of transference phenomena, that is, of where the transference sits for the patient at a particular time. As well, they can be indicators of counter-transference. As we know, breaks yield rich data on fantasies, hopes, disappointments and fears for the analyst and the patient. When I asked one of my analysands, with whom I was unsure about the quality of the therapeutic alliance, how she felt about my upcoming break, she replied, 'I feel nothing. It is just like switching a switch off and on.' Three years into our work together, this patient could finally feel angry at me for going away. I saw this as significant progress in her allowing herself to connect with me in a relational manner – not as someone doing something *to* her, but as someone doing something *with* her. She did not join me in taking pleasure in this advance. Her resistance to seeing herself as dependent on anyone had, of course, been played out in her relationships outside the analysis and was understood as a result of her development being arrested during her practicing sub-phase in response to events that occurred after the birth of a sibling when she was 18 months of age.

Even though all breaks are important windows into transference fantasies, absences by the therapist usually yield the richest material. The break may trigger a memory of the loss through illness or death of a parent, or the reminder of a parent who was never there when the patient needed them. If the patient has had an intrusive parent or sibling, or if they are finding the analysis to be a hardship financially, they may feel a sense of relief when there is a break, but may not express it, for fear of injuring the analyst. Feelings of exclusion from the Oedipal couple, intense jealousy of the analyst's imagined vacation partner, envy of the analyst's ability to take a holiday and presumably enjoy themselves, all may come to the surface in a fresh edition (Usher, 2013). Settlage (1994) analogizes the analytic situation with its breaks and losses and termination to the strange situation: both Mary Main and Settlage tried to understand the child in a situation of being left. If the analyst can empathize and respond appropriately to the patient during times of separation, Settlage states, then 'the patient is able to resume the process of becoming independent which had gone awry during early development' (p. 58).

Lily's (Clinical vignette 2.2) first experience of a break occurred during my summer holiday, which corresponded to her mother's 80th birthday, for which she was expected to have a party. Because Lily's mother lived in a different city, this necessitated her mother staying with her for a number of days. Lily experienced intolerable anxiety leading up to the break, fuelled by her rage at me for abandoning her – which she was unable to even contemplate, as she needed me too much in the face of the anticipated 'onslaught'. She was certain that I was leaving because she was so disgusting and unlovable, which she had suspected all along, but more especially in her present state of helplessness.

During one of our next breaks, about three years into the treatment, Lily's husband became ill and was hospitalized. Once again, I was not there for her. This time, because the illness had not been predicted, she could not allow herself to blame me consciously for the timing of my holiday – it wasn't my 'fault'. However, noticing that she had lost considerable weight and listening to her story, I felt guilty for not having been there. This situation, occurring some time into the treatment, was different from the situation of her mother's visit. Lily could report that she handled it quite well and, indeed, she was beginning to contend with our breaks more and more easily. Growth in this area showed improvement in both self and object constancy.

In analysis in general, and before, during and after breaks in particular, the oscillation between gratification and deprivation is central, as it is in normal development. Analysis is conducted in what Stone (1961, cited in Blatt and Behrends, 1987) calls a state of 'intimate separation' or 'deprivation in intimacy'. The mutative power of analysis derives from the ongoing tension between closeness and distance. Blatt and Behrends agree that gratification must not be totally lost in the frustrations of analysis, but that what is required for change is an oscillation between repeated sequences of gratifying involvement (the patient's feeling understood and seeing the analyst as accepting and empathic) and experienced incompatibility – a finding and a refinding of a good object.

The way the analyst introduces breaks in the treatment and manages the patient's reaction can give valuable information to them about the analyst's encouragement of separation. For myself, having grown up with parents who each had significant separation difficulties, and having been analysed by an analyst who billed me when I attended my mother's funeral out of town, I am undoubtedly oversensitive to the need to give patients their freedom and to not 'punish' them for taking a family holiday or attending a professional conference – i.e. for separating from me and the treatment – by billing them for the absence. I do not recommend this for everyone, but it suits me. Of course, the timing of the breaks (e.g. immediately after beginning treatment; in order to have an affair; or in the midst of a difficult termination) may signal a significant problem in the analytic relationship and must be interpreted. If a patient takes undue advantage of the 'freedom' by being away frequently without good reason, it becomes obvious that the absence is functioning, at least in part, as a resistance to the treatment and requires exploration. As long as this is done in moderation, it can lead to a helpful balance between dependence and independence: the need to be held (back) and the rage at being held back. When the vacation principles are explained to the patient in advance, as, for example, 'It would be best to have as few long interruptions to our work as possible, and therefore, it would be good if you could schedule your holidays at the same time as mine', at least the patient is advised of the more ideal situation and, when there is a therapeutic alliance, will make plans with that in mind. No matter how free everyone is, absences will still significantly affect both parties – particularly the patient – and yield interesting material, both in the anticipation leading up to the break and in the aftermath.

Pauses or breaks in the treatment early on may offer the first indication of unresolved separation issues. Because of their experience of guilt and indebtedness, paired with their resentment and their need to push away – and including their significant need for the therapist – patients with these sorts of difficulties are unusually cautious about the impact they may be having on the therapist. They may fear that their 'unacceptable' emotions are the cause of the break; or, as in the case of Lily, they may imagine that the analyst is taking a vacation just to get rid of them. Their murderous wishes can be thinly covered by their concern for the therapist on their holiday, for example, 'I hope nothing happens to you – take care.' It becomes obvious that breaks highlight the patient's use of defences: observing which defences are summoned to deal with the break, and whether they are archaic or adaptive provides useful information.

Patients with separation difficulties need to know about vacation plans well in advance, the theory being that this gives them the chance to explore their reactions in the treatment – that is, if they can remember that the analyst is leaving, and when. When patients report having shown up at the locked door of the office after the analyst has already gone, or when they do not attend the session before or after a break, thinking the analyst is away, early issues of abandonment by caretakers come into the treatment in painful relief, and may indicate an unconscious attempt to evoke guilt in the analyst, feelings that may or may not have been evoked in the original object(s). A patient's reaction to feelings of being rejected, to being dismissed or forgotten about, to loss – or to just not mattering – may lead to feelings of rage and hopelessness. The mild-mannered Diana, described in Clinical vignette 2.4, who was teased and inhibited in her family of origin, consistently cancelled the first session after my return from a break. She could not imagine that she might be angry, and always had a 'legitimate' reason for the cancellation. Much later in her treatment, when she revealed that she had never been able to see herself as having any anger, she was quite pleased to be able to say the breaks angered her.

The resumption of the treatment after the break requires the analyst to be empathically and emotionally available to the patient – the patient's experience of the analyst as a human being is most helpful here. Settlage (1994) suggests analysing the patient's repressed anger and aggression by calling attention to the absence of anger where anger would be expected – as often these patients are not angry enough – and analysing the patient's defensive inhibitions to giving and receiving love, which have interfered with the development of self and object constancy.

The treatment with Carla (Clinical vignette 2.1) – with its opportunity for separations and reunions – was an example of the ability to resolve earlier separation issues *in vivo*, as it were. We noticed how Carla's symptoms decreased each time after her decision to leave town (and her therapy) was able to be made, and she usually left relatively symptom-free. The resolution of her rapprochement crisis occurred after Carla had completed graduate school and settled in her hometown when we could continue our work in more depth. The remobilization of previously arrested development during separation–individuation time – due, in part, to Carla's mother's absence and to Carla's feeling responsible for the care of her father from very early on – was an integral feature and a powerful therapeutic force in the ongoing work.

Gabbard (2009) reports that it is now commonplace for some patients to engage in a kind of 'intermittent analysis', where they return periodically for analytic work based on difficult life events. Although that does not exactly describe the situation with Carla, it is evident that the breaks in the work with her had a positive, growth-enhancing effect.

There is not a great deal of analytic literature focusing specifically on brief breaks/pauses/interruptions in the treatment. Peck (1961) describes his patients' dreams before and after a break in treatment, stating that very effective work may be stimulated by an interruption in the analysis. He states that the automatic self-analysis that continues within the patient during an interruption may be especially effective because repression has been relaxed. Jackel (1966) describes five cases where an interruption in the treatment led to the emergence of the wish to have a child – for patients of both sexes. He states that this wish appeared in transference acting out, in dreams and in his patients' associations. Kuiper (1970) describes patients' reactions to analysts' vacations as: the inability to synchronize their own vacations with the analyst's; depressive and rage reactions; the tendency to pass on to others the hurt experienced by 'being sent away'; self-punitive tendencies that are reactions to unconscious vengeance and death wishes toward the analyst; and fantasies concerning the analyst's erotic travel adventures. He states that the type of acting out the patient chooses can provide insight into the patient's basic neurotic conflict.

As we know, Freud himself was very structured about his vacations and spent the summers with his family in the mountains – even though he was known to take a patient with him for a brief time under special circumstances. Analysts in the United States followed Freud's example by taking holidays in the month of August. One patient I saw was concerned that I would not remember her after the summer break – not only forget what she had been talking about in the treatment, but not remember actually who she was. Holding on to the differentiated image of another person was difficult for this patient, and she assumed it would be for me as well. The repeated relief of being welcomed back after a separation allowed her to experience significant growth.

In my experience, breaks always seem to come at the 'wrong' time for patients – just when they are undergoing the worst stress, just when they are starting to understand their profound traumatic deprivations, just when they finally feel free enough to free associate. It is always helpful to understand which came first – the announcement of a break or the experience of overwhelming stress. Comparing the transference reaction to breaks annually offers both the patient and the analyst an indication of the therapeutic progress, or lack thereof, in separation–individuation, as well as in other areas.

The jury is out on whether analysts should be *appropriately* available to very distressed patients during breaks. For some patients, the offer of contact when the analyst is away will feel insulting, as if their ability to carry on without treatment is doubtful, and may be an indication of the analyst's unconscious need to hang onto the patient; for some, it may feel like a lifesaver. It will be a different experience for different patients at different times in the treatment, and so analysts must use their judgment. I find that email used for this purpose, with certain patients at certain times, is inherently distant enough, providing both parties with a time lag. My experience has been that almost no one has contacted me during these times, even when I expected they would.

In the case of couples, because they have each other, the transference is not as dense and breaks are usually much easier for all parties, even, perhaps surprisingly, when they are in crisis. They often welcome the opportunity to be on their own.

## Termination

'A patient is nearing the end of a lengthy analysis. The fantasy is that his analyst, who has a pair of tickets to an Isaac Stern concert, offers him one of the tickets as a gift. At the concert hall he sits beside the recipient of the analyst's other ticket, who turns out to be none other than the analyst's lovely, and unmarried, daughter. They talk, they start to date each other, they fall in love, and soon they are happily married – living, of course, not too far from daddy-analyst' (Viorst, 1982, p. 399). Viorst asks, 'A typical patient's fantasy? Not quite. The fantasy belongs not to the patient but to the analyst.'

### The analyst

In her one- to two- hour interviews with 20 analysts (11 supervising and training analysts), Viorst studied the analysts' experience of loss at the end of analysis. During these interviews, the analysts were able to talk about their counter-transference at the approach of termination – the treatment phase, as she says, and I agree, where counter-transference difficulties may play the largest part.

One child analyst stated that he found it hard to accept that some things have to be resolved on one's own, that 'to hold on too long was just as harmful as not holding on at all' (Viorst, 1982, p. 406). A senior analyst spoke of having to renounce the 'very deep pleasure he found in parenting'. One analyst acknowledged she had difficulty letting go of a patient who provided her with a holding environment. Another did not want to lose a patient with a good sense of humour who cheered up her day. Yet another analyst saw that he was playing the loving son with his patient – which he could never do with his own angry father. At termination, the analysts often had to work through the incompleteness of the analysis, and their often too-high expectations of their patients, which can lead to hostility against the patient for the crime of not giving the analyst the narcissistic gratification of being cured.

The analysts were also forced to think about what they had not accomplished in their own analyses – and indeed, how their own analyses terminated. 'For as they let go, in the terminal phase, of some hopes and dreams they have harbored for their patients, they also may finally have to let go of some hopes and dreams they have harbored for themselves' (Viorst, 1982, p. 416).

Viorst talks about the patient going through a kind of rebirth at the end of the treatment into a new life. However, she does not discuss the analysts' feelings of being left behind alone, or their envy of their patient for having had such a good analyst (them). Perhaps this was not emphasized by any of the analysts she interviewed, but as much as we might wish that parents could be like these analysts seem to be, and understand their feelings as the time to separate from their offspring draws near, feelings of painful loss, abandonment, being left, being old, having given 'too much' of oneself and now being drained, along with the envy of youth, may be just too hard in real life. Still the analogy is impressive.

In a more recent article, Gabbard (2009) describes a fantasy while listening to a case report about an infertile patient. The fantasy was that the analysis cured the infertility. I think most analysts are somewhat guilty of such magical, omnipotent thoughts about analysis. (I myself once told a patient who was suffering from uterine fibroids that their origin related to her guilt about an affair she was having – she accepted the interpretation, ended the affair, but the fibroids remained.) The analyst must learn to deal with the imperfections of the treatment at termination – and with his or her overvaluation, or indeed, idealization of psychoanalysis.

Freud (1937), as we know, was not onside with the idealization of psychoanalysis; in fact, quite the contrary. In 'Analysis Terminable and Interminable', published on his 81st birthday, two years before his death, and after he had endured many operations on his mouth and painful prostheses, his pessimism about the therapeutic efficacy of psychoanalysis is clear. Freud stresses the limits of the psychoanalytic technique and the obstacles to a cure. In the editor's introduction, it is noted that his scepticism about the prophylactic power of psychoanalysis extends not only to not preventing the occurrence of a new neurosis but even to not preventing the return of the patient's earlier neurosis.

Putting the paper in further context, Berenstein (1987) adds that Freud had by that time, lost many of his friends and colleagues, including Abraham and Ferenczi. Freud was forced to leave Vienna one year later, leaving behind four of his five sisters, who were murdered at Auschwitz. Perhaps our collective idealization of analytic treatment uses these conditions to excuse Freud's pessimism about the work as we dive harder – and longer – into it. But we begin by degrees to lose our own idealism.

According to Berenstein (1987), Freud was aware that the counter-transference played as decisive a role as the transference in the establishment of a kind of unconscious pact, 'whose observable clinical manifestation is stagnation, whereby the patient fulfils the wish to make the relationship with the analyst *interminable*' (p. 25; emphasis in the original). Even though analyses were relatively brief in Freud's time, Freud was wary of patients lingering too long. His description of his patient Herr E as having a 'career as a patient', and, particularly, his ending with the Wolf Man, whom he describes as a young man 'spoilt by wealth', speaks to the force of the counter-transference.

> Progress came to a stop. We advanced no further in clearing up the neurosis of his childhood, on which his later illness was based, and it was obvious that the patient found his present position highly comfortable and had no wish to take any step forward which would bring him nearer to the end of his treatment. It was a case of the treatment inhibiting itself: it was in danger of failing as a result of its – partial – success. In this predicament I resorted to the heroic measure of fixing a time-limit for the analysis … His resistances shrank up, and in the last months of his treatment he was able to reproduce all the memories and to discover all the connections which seemed necessary for understanding his early neurosis and mastering his present one.
>
> (Freud, 1937, p. 217)

As we see later, this termination was premature.

In comparing the process of separation of adolescents from their parents and the concept of premature termination, Novick (1982) states, 'With their parents and with the therapist, the main impetus is toward a premature termination by, for example, running away, being thrown out, or moving away because of some external pressure, such as going to university' (p. 335). Freud's ending with the Wolf Man seems to fall into the category of 'being thrown out', although it stood the Wolf Man in good stead for some years.

Most analysts and long-term psychodynamic therapists would agree that termination is a crucial part of the therapeutic work, and that there are significant benefits to the conduct of a termination phase, although perhaps not like that of Freud's with the Wolf Man. Novick (1982) states that one precondition for a terminal phase is the patient's capacity to observe the transference rather than live it out as a current reality. In the ideal, mutually agreed upon termination, both the analyst and the patient come to the conclusion that the therapeutic goals have been achieved, within the limitations of the technique and the patient's personality. This implies that both the patient and the analyst have let go, as much as possible, of the fantasy of cure and are able to metaphorically pat each other and themselves on the back for the work done. Resolving the rapprochement crisis in the analysis in a satisfying manner leaves the patient with a feeling of acceptance rather than of being bereft or angry.

Gabbard (2009) states, 'Termination presents both parties with an extraordinary challenge … In real life, of course, an intense relationship involving love and profound attachment is brought to an end only by death, or by extraordinary rage or narcissistic injury' (p. 579). He cites the example of a colleague who confided that he and his patient had a therapeutic relationship characterized by humour and caring, in addition to good analytic work. This colleague said he felt like Henry Higgins in *My Fair Lady*; he had worked with her to the point where she was successful, and now he could not let her go. He even added, 'I've grown accustomed to her face'. In consultation with Gabbard, this analyst recognized that his rationale for the patient's needing more time to function independently represented 'both an erotic longing for the patient and a view of her as a narcissistic extension of himself that he could not sever' (p. 588). The part about the narcissistic extension echoes a parent's perspective when having to let go of a valued child. As we can see from Viorst's work, and as we know in ourselves, it is such for both parties, parents and analysts.

Craige (2006) cites Davies' notion that termination is not just a long goodbye, but a multitude of goodbyes that come from multiple levels of development and sometimes different centres of trauma – for both the patient and the analyst. Quoting Davies, she says, 'Each [goodbye] holds the potential not only for growth, emergence, and liberation, but also for grief, despair, and narcissistic collapse' (p. 585).

Novick (1982) states that during the termination phase, the analyst qua analyst becomes more revealed, but usually not the analyst as a real person. However, over the course of time, the patient gains in reality for the analyst. Novick states that at termination it is the analyst as a transference object who is mourned. Therefore, it is the analyst, rather than the patient, who experiences the loss of a 'real' object at termination. A terminating patient remarked to him that probably he would miss her more than she would miss him. 'I agreed with her' (p. 355). We know our patients as people and they know us as analysts; children, until they are quite grown, do not know their parents as individuals – and sometimes they never do. The pre-termination and termination phases are almost as clear in family life as they are in analysis, if we are attuned to them, as children prepare to leave the nest, although they may not be mutually agreed upon. The experience of sending someone out into the world who has needed and depended on one's intimate caretaking, and of renting their room, or their therapeutic hour, to someone else – even metaphorically – may be one of life's hardest tasks. (One place where the analogy does not hold, however, is that parents are faced with the often Herculean task of incorporating a stranger – and one who is, no doubt, having sex with their son or daughter – into the family circle and around the dinner table.) The goals are surprisingly the same, however, if both the parent and the analyst can let go – a wish for the person to develop the capacity for post-analytic self-analysis, the ability to internalize the good qualities of the analyst/parent and to live an independent, satisfying life.

In a later article, Novick (1997) states that there is something in the reaction of therapists to the end of treatment that seriously interferes with their conceiving of termination and thus interferes with working through their own mourning. The process of relinquishing omnipotent fantasies and confronting the narcissistic counter-transference as we face the limitations of our theory and technique is, perhaps, understandably, resisted by most therapists.

Each time someone leaves, even when they express a moving statement of gratitude, there is a loss for both, in therapy as it is in families.

### The patient

Melanie Klein (1950) relates the ending of analysis to very early experience: 'It has often been observed that the termination of an analysis reactivates in the patient earlier situations of parting, and is in the nature of a weaning experience' (p. 78). She states that even if satisfactory results have been achieved (capacity for love, object relations and work), the termination of an analysis is bound to stir up painful feelings: it amounts to a state of mourning.

Does knowing the analyst as a real person make it easier or more difficult to separate? If the idealization of the analyst in adult treatment is not resolved, patients may want to maintain the blissful state – to avoid growing up or because they sense this is what the analyst needs. Candidates often have the experience of reconnecting with their analyst as a colleague – in meetings or on committees. If the analyst is being real, the idealizing transference will be strained, at best; however, transference persists for a very long time.

With parents, healthy separation may be made easier, as truly knowing the parents may allow the child to forgive them, identify with them and thus feel closer to them in a *different* way. This can have a positive effect in resolving the rapprochement crisis. On the other hand, if the growing person learns that parents are truly in need, he or she then has the additional task of devising a way of being there and yet continuing to separate, so that there is minimal pain of guilty abandonment. Patients such as Carla (Clinical vignette 2.1), who have grown up feeling they must look after a parent or parents, often feel the same about their analyst; no surprise here. Both of us anticipated Carla's reluctance to end her treatment. I needed to reassure her that I was fine without her. The post-analytic contact, however, initiated by her and described in the next section, was a relief to both of us.

In her article described earlier, Erreich (2011) writes,

> In a particularly poignant hour, one of our last, Nick [a five-year-old patient] was describing how baby alligators get dangerous as they get bigger and can kill people. ... It seemed that Nick was worried about killing me off via his anticipated termination ... Nick commented that he wanted to finish up some things with me, like a fishing-rod project ... and he asked me who I thought was the stronger of us. I said I didn't know, what did he think? Nick replied he was stronger and smarter.
>
> (Erriech, 2011, p. 134)

Erreich states that this example of Nick's ending treatment demonstrated the intermingling of Oedipal guilt, survivor guilt and separation guilt that beset our patients when they are struggling with separation–individuation during the termination phase.

Lily's (Clinical vignette 2.2) termination, after ten years of analysis, involved her in months of agonizing decision-making. She set dates and changed them twice, as she needed to feel certain that it was she who wanted to leave, that I was not trying to eject her, that it was fine for her to end her treatment, and that both of us would survive. At one point, after the first date had been tentatively set, Lily asked me what she was like when she first came to see me. I described, as best I could, my impressions of her at that time – in what seemed like so many years ago. She said she noticed that I took notes and asked if she could read them. Because I often write comments in the margin, and also because I wanted control over what would be read, I compromised by saying I would read the notes to her. She was delighted with this and sat up cross-legged on the couch to listen. Since she (and her brother) had never been read to as children, this inadvertently fulfilled a need that had been unattended to in the analysis. She did not require the reading for very long and felt satisfied that she had made good use of the analysis. As she ended, she was still left with her fear that I would not continue to worry about her and that I would forget her. My continuing to worry about her was still, unfortunately, more important than my being proud of her, as one of the rare ways her mother expressed her love for her was to worry about her, and she felt protected by my worrying. Her fear that I would forget her was a sign of her still wobbly object constancy.

Balint (1950), writing of the last session, states, 'Usually the patient leaves after the last session happy but with tears in his eyes – and, I think I may admit – the analyst is in a very similar mood' (p. 197).

### Couples

In terminating with couples, one complication that was mentioned in Chapter 3 is that sometimes partners are not at the same developmental/ psychological level; thus, one may be ready to terminate ahead of the other. Interpretations regarding how each sees termination – for example, anxiety or guilt about achieving independence as a separate couple, particularly in terms of leaving parents behind – can be very productive. The termination of Pamela and Tom, who ended their relationship in the session, has been described in Clinical vignette 3.1.

Because couples have each other to talk to, they may discuss plans for termination outside the session. In one couple I saw several years ago, it became obvious to all of us that one partner was very uncomfortable in the treatment, not liking to talk. After several months of work during which I felt there was some halting progress, the partners announced to me that the session they were currently attending would be their last! Straining to adhere to Bion's dictum of the analyst approaching each session without memory or desire, I sat in silence, trying not to look desirous. The male partner explained that this was a gift to his wife (now smiling) to end the therapy, because she found it so stressful. Teaching him empathy seems to have been overdone.

As can be seen, strong counter-transference feelings and fantasies, which include being excluded from the Oedipal couple (e.g. above), are often evoked in the therapist during a couple's termination phase. How much of a holding environment has been provided in both directions? What or whom did the couple represent for the therapist and what does saying goodbye to them mean? Did the therapist have the opportunity to fix his or her parents? Or to be parented by them? Or is the therapist relieved to see these warring people leave and to restore quiet to the office? Termination with couples has been described in detail in an earlier publication (Usher, 2008).

As in individual therapy, the couples therapist's unresolved issues of separation bubble up to the surface during the termination phase; perhaps 'bubble up' is too gentle a way of putting it – as in some individual terminations, it is more like an active volcano. Is the therapist able to let the couple go? Several times in my practice, I have had the thought, 'I will really miss them'. I thought this way about Nate and Caroline (Clinical vignette 3.2), as they were preparing to leave. With Pamela and Tom (Clinical vignette 3.1), as has been mentioned, their last session was a very sad one, as it was then that their final decision to end their marriage was made. They did not want to let go of each other, and I did not want to let go of them. Had the treatment failed? Or was it a success because they were able to part? My feelings of sadness were related to Pamela's experience of loss and also to my knowledge that I would not ever see them again. (My policy with couples is not to treat them individually before or after they have been in couples therapy with me.)

What is having to be relinquished and mourned for the *couple* in ending is not so much the therapist, but the holding environment with the 'new' parent that was created by all three participants – which allowed them to talk, confidentially and safely, about private and difficult matters. There is a difference in the intensity of the bereavement for the therapist compared to the ending in individual therapy. The partners have each other with whom to ride off into the sunset; the therapist is left behind. Depending on the therapist's satisfaction in their extra-work life, and their own close relationships, this can be very difficult and may stir up envy and even resentment. Like when a child leaves home, the state of the parents' marriage and their satisfaction with their own lives, matters – really matters.

Freud makes a convincing case for the analyst's awareness of his reaction to different stages of the analysis.

Among the factors which influence the prospects of analytic treatment, and add to its difficulties in the same manner as the resistances, must be reckoned not only the nature of the patient's ego, but the individuality of the analyst … The special conditions of analytic work do actually cause the analyst's own defects to interfere with his making a correct assessment of the state of things in his patient … But where and how is the poor wretch to acquire the ideal qualifications which he will need in his profession? The answer is, in an analysis of himself.

(Freud, 1937, pp. 247–248)

And thus, as we know, analysis interminable was born.

## Post-analytic contact

I happened to have lunch, during the writing of this chapter, with a retired colleague and friend. 'I heard from one of my control cases', she said, smiling, and happily relayed the gist of the letter (an actual letter). She was obviously pleased that her patient remembered her and chose to keep her informed about her life.

Hartlaub et al. (1986) conducted a study of graduates of the Denver Psychoanalytic Society, asking for their experience with patients making contact with them after the analysis. They reported that within three years of termination, two-thirds of 'successfully analysed' patients had re-contacted them. They surveyed 71 cases and found that most contacts were brief and did not seem to be the result of incomplete analysis. They were related to needs for the continuing de-idealization of the analyst; the reactivation of the self-analytic function; and the restructuring of self- and object representations, by reporting developmentally significant accomplishments. The therapist's acknowledgement appeared to be an integral part of the restructuring.

Even though this is an early study, it probably represents quite accurately the situation today. Re-contact after termination is one of the factors demonstrating that the ultimate severance of Oedipal ties, the relinquishment of the analyst, is always very hard, and may not even be necessary for happy functioning.

We know from the studies done by Schachter (1990, 1992) and Schachter and Brauer (2001) that post-termination contact between patients and analysts occurs frequently, initiated, of course, by the patient. Unlike the Menninger Follow-Up Study and other studies initiated for research, here the focus is on the patient's need to initiate post-termination contact: they may need to make sure the analyst is still alive, they may need refuelling from the analyst, or they may unconsciously sense the analyst's need to hear from them. Schachter's 1990 study demonstrated that when analysands could not re-contact their analyst, usually because the analyst had since died, they could not fully mourn the end of the analysis. Patients needed the experience of the analyst as a real person for mourning to occur. Those analysands who were left with a definite sense of their analyst as a real person, gave the clearest evidence of a full-blown transference relationship and experienced the most intensely felt mourning.

Craige (2006), cited earlier, states that our patients actually tie off most of the loose ends that may appear during termination *after* they leave us. There is life after termination, after all, and a most intellectually interesting one it is – just as there is exciting life after leaving home.

Carla, described earlier, emailed me photos of her home and her baby after our time together, needing my reassurance that it was good for her to continue growing and benefitting from the knowledge that I was not suffering because of it. She knew, also, that I would be happy to hear from her. Lily emailed me updates of her progress, but still tended to qualify/ undo her achievements with self-deprecating comments. She needed to feel she was still in my mind and that I still worried about her, at least a little. Sometimes these contacts occur quite soon after termination and then fizzle out. Sometimes, as with one couple I saw over an exceedingly stressful period of their lives together, ritual holiday cards are sent for years after – complete with photos. One patient I saw more than ten years ago still writes at Christmas time, updating me about her life. This patient, working in a helping profession, was able to make use of a relatively brief treatment in a way that was especially important to her and for which she was especially grateful. Most analysts (and parents) enjoy this kind of contact. But, unlike with the patient's parents, I have yet to hear how I ruined someone's life with the treatment.

In talking about the analyst's part in keeping, rather than holding, the patient, we are reminded that analysts are well-known for their tendency to work until they are carried out of their offices feet first. Consider the title of Kurt Eissler's (2013) essay, 'Psychoanalyst: A Profession for an Immortal?'. Schwartz and Silver's (1990) edited book contains 'confessions' by well-known analysts about their falling ill; we can see very clearly their tendency to deny any illness and to keep working, sometimes despite obvious limitations – also, unfortunately, obvious to their patients. In his 100th birthday speech, Martin S. Bergman (quoted in Junkers, 2013) said, 'I remain thankful to psychoanalysis for protecting me from an early retirement and the swimming pools of Florida, and for enabling me to still work and teach at the age of 100 and still make discoveries and write.'

If we add to this sentiment unresolved separation issues in the therapist's history, we have a situation where unsuspecting patients can leave only at their peril. The parent needs to parent, the analyst needs to analyse, but do patients need to be patients?

## Quotable quote

H. Craige (2002): *'What I lost … it's immeasurable really, a relationship with someone who knew more about me than anyone else in my life, who was completely committed to understanding me.'*

## References

Balint, M. (1950). On the termination of analysis. *International Journal of Psychoanalysis, 30*, 196–199.

Berenstein, I. (1987). Analysis terminable and interminable, fifty years on. *International Journal of Psychoanalysis, 68*, 21–35.

Blatt, S. J. and R. S. Behrends (1987). Internalization, separation–individuation, and the nature of therapeutic action. *International Journal of Psychoanalysis, 68*, 279–297.

Craige, H. (2002). Mourning analysis: The post-termination phase. *Journal of the American Psychoanalytic Association, 50*(2), 508–550.

Craige, H. (2006). Termination, terminable and interminable. *Psychoanalytic Dialogues, 16*(5), 585–590.

Eissler, K. (2013). Psychoanalyst: A profession for an immortal? In G. Junkers (Ed.) (2013). *The empty couch: The taboo of ageing and retirement in psychoanalysis.* London: Routledge.

Erreich, A. (2011). More than enough guilt to go around: Oedipal guilt, survivor guilt, separation guilt. *Journal of the American Psychoanalytic Association, 59*(1), 131–151.

Freud, S. (1937). *Analysis terminable and interminable,* S. E. 23.

Gabbard, G. O. (2009). What is a 'good enough' termination? *Journal of the American Psychoanalytic Association, 57*(3), 575–594.

Hartlaub, G. H., G. C. Martin and M. W. Rhine (1986). Recontact with the analyst following termination: A survey of seventy-one cases. *Journal of the American Psychoanalytic Association, 34*, 895–910.

Jackel, M. M. (1966). Interruptions during psychoanalytic treatment and the wish for a child. *Journal of the American Psychoanalytic Association, 14*, 730–735.

Junkers, G. (Ed.) (2013). *The empty couch: The taboo of ageing and retirement in psychoanalysis*. London: Routledge.

Klein, M. (1950). On the criteria for the termination of an analysis. *International Journal of Psychoanalysis, 31*, 78–80.

Kuiper, P. C. (1970). The analyst's vacations. *International Journal of Psychoanalysis, 24*(1–6), 525.

Novick, J. (1982). Termination: Themes and issues. *Psychoanalytic Inquiry, 2*, 329–365.

Novick, J. (1997). Termination conceivable and inconceivable. *Psychoanalytic Psychology, 14*, 145–162.

Peck, J. S. (1961). Dreams and interruptions in the treatment. *Psychoanalytic Quarterly, 30*, 209–220.

Schachter, J. (1990). Post-termination patient-analyst contact: I Analysts' attitudes and experience; II Impact on patients. *International Journal of Psychoanalysis, 71*, 475–485.

Schachter, J. (1992). Concepts of termination and post-termination patient–analyst contact. *International Journal of Psychoanalysis, 73*, 137–154.

Schachter, J. and L. Brauer (2001). The effect of the analyst's gender and other factors on post-termination patient–analyst contact: Confirmation by a questionnaire study. *International Journal of Psychoanalysis, 82*, 1123–1132.

Schwartz, H. J. and A. L. S. Silver (Eds.) (1990). *Illness in the analyst: Implications for the treatment relationship*. Madison, CT: International Universities Press.

Settlage, C. F. (1994). On the contribution of separation–individuation theory to psychoanalysis: Developmental process, pathogenesis, therapeutic process, and technique. In S. Kramer and S. Akhtar (Eds.), *Mahler and Kohut: Perspectives on development, psychopathology, and technique* (pp. 17–52). Northvale, NJ: Jason Aronson.

Usher, S. F. (2008). *What is this thing called love? A guide to psychoanalytic psychotherapy with couples*. London: Routledge.

Usher, S. F. (2013). *Introduction to psychodynamic psychotherapy technique*, 2nd edn. London: Routledge.

Viorst, J. (1982). Experience of loss at the end of analysis: The analyst's response to termination. *Psychoanalytic Inquiry, 2*, 399–418.

# Chapter 6

# Conclusion

## You can go home again (if you resolve your rapprochement crisis)

At the beginning of the first episode of *The Sopranos*, Tony Soprano (played by James Gandolfini) sits in a psychiatrist's waiting room, doubtful about getting help for his panic attacks. For the informed audience, we think of the panic he experiences as a manifestation of his intrapsychic conflict between some sort of ethics and his propensity to murder people. But Tony is also obviously suffering from significant separation issues in relation to his borderline mother, Livia (played by Nancy Marchand), a cagey, manipulative matriarch, who projects her own thinly concealed rage into her son, spending many of her waking hours plotting to have him killed. In this environment, Tony can never resolve his rapprochement crisis. The 'family' – his family of origin and his work family – consumes his psychic space. Separation from either family would be seen as a crime – probably with fatal consequences.

Family businesses, family cottages, family money, even family traditions (e.g. the Friday or Sunday night dinner) may provide a welcome secure feeling, or may be experienced as a burden where a performance for parents, in-laws and/or siblings is required. Some people can be themselves only in the context of their families. Some cannot be themselves only in this context. In an attempt to create a boundary that individualizes them, the latter group cannot let their families of origin into their real life – to confide about successes or failures. As has been documented, people struggling with separation often present with symptoms of anxiety, panic attacks, depression and a feeling of hopelessness about ever having a good and satisfying life. Again, the patients described here did not, for the most part, come into therapy complaining that they needed to separate from their parents or caretakers. However, as we explored more deeply, these unresolved issues were identified as contributing to the obstruction of their progress in life. Because these specific issues – and their fantasied exhilarating/terrifying consequences – may be unconscious, the therapist will frequently be involved in identifying and naming the latent conflict for the patient, who may not have even realized that they are entitled to struggle for a separate life. As with most important problems in analytic therapy, these issues will come to the surface again and again, sometimes vaguely, sometimes in sharp relief, before the patient ceases being surprised by them, acknowledges them as major inhibiting conflicts and begins to work on them analytically.

I am in agreement with Blatt and Behrends (1987) that the 'mutative factors in psychoanalysis occur within the relationship established between the patient and analyst, and that it is this relational context that provides the patient with the opportunity to explore and to change' (p. 279). I am also in agreement with Busch (2013), who states, in his introduction, 'While the analyst's expertise is crucial to the process, the analyst's stance is primarily one of helping the patient *find his own mind*, rather than mainly being an expert on the content of the patient's mind' (p. xv; emphasis in the original).

As their narratives unfold, it becomes clear that failure-to-completely-launch patients need permission to be their own person and to know that they can stop atoning for their imagined sins vis-à-vis their parents. As has been mentioned throughout, the analyst qua analyst, in real time, naturally becomes involved in giving permission. This is done by the way we raise our eyebrows in disbelief (metaphorically if the patient is on the couch) over what we are hearing when patients describe the Faustian bargain they have made with their families, or in our choice of times to be silent when listening to certain material, or in outright questioning of belief systems (e.g. in a couple I saw, where one partner assumed his parent could live with them, while the other suffered in 'silence'). We may use joking, if it is appropriate, to enlist patients' observing egos, or we can point out the predictability in their troubled relationship with a parent. Seeing the relationship as predictable is beneficial in shoring up the person's adult self and helping them to feel more in control. In seemingly more intractable situations, the use of cognitive behavioural techniques can be helpful – maybe not so much in the actual mechanics as in the implied legitimizing of the weaning process for both parties in terms of frequency of contact, if that is needed.

The permission-giving role of the analyst also includes encouragement for the patient to examine their own, previously denied, need for their parent or sibling. This is a difficult admission for many people to come upon, as all their energy has been directed to the neediness or abuse of/by the parent or sibling; they are the innocent victims. Once this has come into the work, the patient and therapist can begin to untangle the enmeshment and get a clearer picture of who's doing what to whom. In the case of Lily (Clinical vignette 2.2), this was particularly difficult to uncover, as her fragile ego and sense of self needed the story to remain just as she had told it or she would feel unsupported.

Much of what we know about the counter-transference with patients of this sort confirms that the strong tendency is for the therapist to be the good object – unlike the limiting parent(s) – especially since that is congruent with our sense of where things should head. We know that the stakes are high, and it is tempting to nudge things along. However, if the therapist rushes to this stance, the patient's expression of feelings that have existed inside them for a long time becomes short-circuited, as does their mourning the loss of the internalized bad – or good – object.

The parental transference can evince a patient's guilt over imagined sacrifices the analyst may have made for them (e.g. 'I hope you had a chance to have lunch'). This has been discussed earlier. Patients who previously needed permission from mothers or fathers who were unable or unwilling to give it are often surprised that it is imperative for them to, as Modell says, have a right to a life. A patient, a university professor, whom I saw recently, had heard often how her mother had been unable to complete a PhD, implying that the patient's childhood demands prevented it. This patient, although she obtained a PhD, had great difficulty advancing further in her professional life. The key components of the transference were her rage at her mother and her envy of me, whom she imagined had an easily successful professional life.

Because they do not know differently, most of my female patients assume that vocational achievement has been easy for me. However, I will confess that when Diana (Clinical vignette 2.4 and Chapter 4) – the mild-mannered artist who had been aggressively teased by her older brother – asked me how I managed to get as far as I had (implying – at my age), I disclosed to her that I did not tell my family (of origin) when I was completing my PhD, a tactic that made that task easier for me. Self-disclosure is not one of my treatment techniques; but in this case, I felt Diana was using me appropriately as a developmental object. As Settlage

(1994) has said, 'Therapeutic process and developmental process are complementary and proceed hand-in-hand' (p. 40). Diana was able to make use of this normalizing information from the analyst qua analyst, outside of the parental transference.

In terms of the use of splitting, as has been seen in some of the examples described, the idealizing, positive transference is manifested as perceiving the analyst as encouraging separation, compared to the clinging parent(s). In the negative transference, the analyst becomes the depriving, limiting parent – one whose needs must be considered ahead of the patient's. Angry feelings come to the fore as the patient experiences the analyst as not letting them succeed, as being threatened by their intelligence and talents, and as needing to hold on to them. This can be covered by a false compliance and pseudo-idealization. It is exciting to be witness to the breaking up of these defences, as the patient starts to realize that the analyst understands and can accept their negative feelings.

Because of their unconscious guilt about the wish to leave/murder their parents, some failure-to-completely-launch patients may have a tendency to develop a negative therapeutic reaction. They do not allow themselves to progress in treatment – partly as a punishment of themselves and of their analyst, and partly because they do not feel entitled to having a successful analysis and life – a fear of flying too close to the sun. The uneasy relationship that evolves may take some time for both parties to understand.

Although the role of specific underlying trauma in these patients has not been emphasized here, it deserves mention. Have patients for whom these issues are the most salient always suffered traumatic experiences in their early lives? I believe that specific early childhood trauma does not have to be present and, in fact, may be noticeable by its absence – unless we refer to poor 'maternal' caretaking in early life as distinct trauma, or we talk about parental abandonment – which leads to enforced separation. What does have to be present is major stumbling some time before rapprochement; the reasons for this are sometimes unclear. Of course, early trauma – for example, sexual exploitation – leads to inhibitions in growing up, and hence difficulties in separating from one's family of origin, but that is not the focus of this book. The patients described here identified parental neglectful experiences, experiences of being inappropriately co-opted by a parent, feeling the need to care for a parent, or being aggressively teased and bullied by a sibling – all of which they had become aware of during latency, pre-adolescence or later. Of course, these experiences must have been rooted in earlier times, but the memories, and therefore the effects, of these experiences, were, for the most part, linked to post-Oedipal years.

This book is mainly 'white' writing, for which I apologize. Research into separation in other cultures and different religions is a necessary endeavour, and would contribute a great deal to our understanding of those differences not explored here.

I have attempted to update the work of Margaret Mahler, not in the sense of bringing it up to date, but in the sense of relating it to adult life. Issues of separation–individuation are as inevitable in the lives of adults as they are important in early infancy. Beyond Freud's metaphor of the analyst as sculptor, the analyst can be seen as releasing new development in the adult patient, expecting development, encouraging developmental initiatives and acknowledging the patient's developmental achievements. The hope here is that analysts and analytic therapists will listen more attentively to their patients' descriptions of these kinds of obstacles to their having a full and satisfying adult life.

Analytic therapy is a re-finding of old objects and a resumption of early development – in a different and self-encouraging way. In the work with these patients, the push and pull, the advance and retrenchment, of the therapeutic work becomes central. Psychoanalysis moves like the knight in chess – forward and then to the side, never in a straight line – much like development.

## References

Blatt, S. J. and R. S. Behrends (1987). Internalization, separation–individuation, and the nature of therapeutic action. *International Journal of Psychoanalysis, 68*, 279–297.

Busch, F. (2013). *Creating a psychoanalytic mind.* New York: Routledge.

Settlage, C. F. (1994). On the contribution of separation–individuation theory to psychoanalysis: Developmental process, pathogenesis, therapeutic process, and technique. In S. Kramer and S. Akhtar (Eds.), *Mahler and Kohut: Perspectives on development, psychopathology, and technique* (pp. 17–52). Northvale, NJ: Jason Aronson.

# Index

For Product Safety Concerns and Information please contact our EU
representative  GPSR@taylorandfrancis.com
Taylor & Francis Verlag GmbH, Kaufingerstraße 24, 80331 München, Germany

www.ingramcontent.com/pod-product-compliance
Lightning Source LLC
Chambersburg PA
CBHW070349270326
41926CB00017B/4060

9 7 8 1 1 3 8 6 5 8 2 7 1